Breakfast with the FBI

By

Erina Bridget Ring

Breakfast with the FBI

For my children

*With grateful thanks to my husband, Jack, and my good friend
Carolyn Woolston for their constant support.*

Prologue

"Rose Ryan?"

"Yes? I am Rose Ryan."

A tall, thin man in his forties sat down across from me and pinned me with an intent look. "My name is Scott Aiden. I'm with the FBI."

My heart dropped into my stomach. "Oh, my God, the FBI? Really?"

He nodded and pushed his ID badge across the table. I couldn't look at it; I could only look at him. He wore wire-rimmed glasses and a dark grey suit, but what did I know? What did FBI agents usually wear? Finally I looked down at his badge, and then back at him.

You don't have a choice, Rose, I thought. *You went to the police, and . . . and . . . Oh, God, I was trapped.*

"Mrs. Ryan?"

I sucked in my breath. "Yes, Mr. -- "

"Just Scott," he said with a slight smile. "I think maybe you should start at the beginning."

So I did.

Chapter One

I looked up from my teller's window to see a young man, a turtleneck rolled up over his mouth, standing next to the counter along the far side of the bank wall. That was odd, I thought. And then suddenly he pulled a gun out of his pants pocket.

"Everything will be okay," he yelled. "Just do what I tell you!"

I froze. After being a stay-at-home mom for 17 years, ever since Jim and I were married, I'd gone to work. I had only had this job a short while and I didn't want to lose it . . . and I didn't want to die!

Shaking, I managed to press my finger on the button underneath the counter, which sends an alarm directly to the police department. The teller next to me asked, "What do you want us to do?" Her voice cracked when she spoke.

"Take out all your money! Then put it in that burlap bag at the back of the counter, over there."

I looked toward the counter and the man shouted, "You!" He pointed his gun straight at me. "You! Do it! Quickly!"

I couldn't help staring at him. He had steel blue eyes with pinpoint pupils, and I noticed he wore a silver and black watch on his left arm and a silver band on his left hand. The gun was black.

He started to fidget and pace, pointing the gun first at me, then at the tellers on either side of me. *Stay calm*, I told myself. *Don't shout or make any sudden moves.*

The teller on my left whispered, "What do you want us to do now?"

"Get that bag and put all the money in it and give it to her." He pointed his gun at me. *Oh, God. Keep calm. Get the bag and don't drop it. Just do what he says.* I scrambled to open my teller drawer, grabbed the bag, and shoved in all the cash, including the bills that were marked in case of a robbery.

"Now," he shouted, "All of you, get down on the floor and don't follow me out. Get down! And stay down!"

I lay down on the floor with the other two tellers. "Stay down, you guys," I murmured, and I prayed hard that he couldn't hear me. Then I heard the bank door close and we waited for the police to come. Finally I reached up for the phone and dialed 911, fearing the panic button had not alerted the police.

"We've been robbed," I whispered. "It just happened at the Harvest Bank, and the gunman left, but he may still be out front. He said to lie in the floor and we're afraid to get up for fear he's out there. Please hurry."

We stayed down on the floor for what seemed an eternity. One teller started to cry, and I resolved I would keep it together until the police came. When they arrived, we were all still lying on the floor. I was face down. One teller was crying. The police officer said it was okay to get up, but one teller was so panic-stricken she couldn't move.

They asked each of us for a description, and we all had a different picture of the man. I was shaken but I could still talk, and I described him as I remembered.

A day later, at our weekly meeting, I was commended on giving such a complete description. The robber was arrested the next day, trying to hold up another bank 30 miles away.

It took me a week to stop shaking every time a man approached my teller window. From that day on, I was terrified of guns.

They had hired me at the bank right away, and I liked my job, even though my first day was an eye-opener. The Harvest bank was a trim-looking grey and white building on the east side of town, with perfectly manicured shrubbery in front and curving brick steps up to the entrance. From the outside it looked inviting, like someone's home. Inside it was clean and airy with light shades of grey and white and darker grey accents on walls that served as partitions. The floors were marbled tile with soft grey carpet under the managers' desks, which were dark mahogany with black leather chairs.

Inside it was quiet (usually), with green ficus trees in the lobby and vases of flowers in the customer area. Photos of pastures and corn fields and old tractors decorated the walls, including pictures of the farmers who had built the town.

One day about a week after the robbery, the lines were extra-long since it was the 15th of the month, a payday. We usually had five tellers, but that morning it dawned on me there were only three of us. Dana and Kim were absent. I thought that was strange because they'd both been here that morning, so I asked Carol.

"Where are Dana and Kim?"

"They were let go."

I gasped. "Really?"

"Really. Rose, I can't talk about this right now. We'll discuss this in a group meeting at the end of the day, after everyone balances."

When 5 o'clock finally came, Carol locked the front doors and announced, "All of you, balance quickly and come to my desk. We need to talk about something."

My supervisor, Carol, was a smart woman in her late fifties with dark hair. She usually dressed in dark suits. She had a way of defusing tense situations, especially when it came to currency errors at the end of the day when the tellers had to balance their money drawers.

Everyone took Carol seriously. When it came to numbers she was the best at finding errors, and even the top officers at the bank regarded her with respect. So when she said something, you listened.

By ten after five I was balanced to the penny, but Deanna and Gerri were struggling. I went over and asked if they needed help.

Deanna was desperate. "Please don't say anything out loud," she said under her breath. "I'm five thousand dollars off."

"You can't be," I answered quietly. I took her transaction receipts for the day and immediately found the error. "Here, you just transposed five thousand dollars for fifty dollars."

"Oh, thank you, Rose. I'll keep my job another day!"

I turned to Gerri, who did not look happy. Apparently she wasn't balancing, either. It turned out she was $100 short. She looked at me with panic in her eyes. "Here are my transactions receipts for the day; would you go through them while I re-count my money?"

"Don't forget to count your coins in the lower vault," I said. Then I added, "Gerri, did you have any out-of-the-vault transactions?"

"No."

I went through her tape and everything looked fine. Then I started to re-count her cash, and when I picked up the money drawer, I found a $100 bill just sitting there all by itself. "Gerri, here's your missing hundred dollars."

"Oh, Rose, I wonder how that happened?"

Before I could answer, Carol called to us from across the room. "It's getting late and I need to speak to all of you. Put your money drawers away and come over to my desk."

We all lined up at the vault and one by one we checked out. Then we moved in front of Carol's desk.

"This meeting will be brief and to the point," she began. "We lost two tellers today due to daily shortages in their balances. The bank will not tolerate this. Any shortage over twenty dollars in a single month is too much. If this occurs, you will be terminated."

We all looked at each other. I knew that Dana and Kim had been let go because of shortages; none of us were privy to how short they were, but I knew they constantly struggled to balance every day.

Carol looked at us with a somber expression on her narrow face. "Tomorrow some changes will be made. Rose, from now on you will be head teller. Charlene will be learning the new ATM system, and when she finishes her training she will show Rose and Mike and me. Deanna, you need to balance every day for a full month, and then you will learn all the bank procedures."

Deanna looked relieved. Gina's name was the only one not mentioned. Then I noticed that Mike, the chief financial officer, was standing at the back of the room, listening. I wondered what he was thinking.

Mike then spoke up. "The president wants to meet with all the tellers upstairs in his office." This made me really nervous. But when we all got upstairs, the bank president, Fredric, started talking about dressing like professionals, making sure our clothes were not too suggestive. Under her breath, Deanna murmured, "Whoo, whoo," which I thought very inappropriate. We all turned to look at her, and she got the message to just listen and not comment.

By then Fredric was directing his remarks at just Deanna. She was embarrassed and kept looking down at her skirt, tugging it to make it longer. Then she grabbed her hair and started to fiddle with it.

"We are a professional bank," Fredric said, looking at her. "We will all dress accordingly."

When the meeting was adjourned, Deanna walked past me and muttered, "Mary Poppins here doesn't need to worry about her dressing." With a jolt I realized she was talking about me!

4

I was wearing a peach crepe de chine blouse with a silky bow, tucked into a pale green wool skirt that came just to my knees, plain black pumps, and nylons. My hair was neatly done and I always wore tasteful jewelry, nothing too flashy. I wanted to look professional. More than that, I wanted to *be* professional.

Every morning I woke up at 5:30 a.m., took a walk with the dogs, showered and dressed in my "success" outfit, and drove to work with a real sense of accomplishment. I loved my job. I was learning fast, and I was always pleasant to my customers. I knew how to run the teller line and how to balance the branch vault and I was being shown the ins and outs of loan documentation. I'd always liked the prospect of learning about mortgages and loans; I was beginning to think about running a small branch myself.

We had just opened an ATM where people could withdraw their money from outside the bank. This was something new, and soon I would learn to balance one of those. I could hardly wait.

Chapter Two

That evening when I got home Jim had already picked up the kids from their after-school activities. Our children were in high school, both high achievers who thrived on challenges. Margaret excelled in math and science and played soccer. Anthony was a whiz with math and computers, and he played baseball. I used to wonder where they got their taste for tackling difficult projects, but looking back on it now, I can understand.

I told Jim about the two tellers who had been fired and that I had been made head teller at the main branch.

My husband grinned at me. "Sounds like you'll be able to run the whole thing on your own soon."

Inside I knew he was right; I did want to run a branch on my own some day. I was really good at my job, and it looked like the bank was growing. I'd heard that a small branch might open up on the edge of town. I couldn't wait until that happened.

The kids cleared the dishes and got started on their homework, and I sat down with Jim and turned on the TV. Almost as soon as he reclined his chair, he was sound asleep.

Jim worked long hours as an engineer, and he often brought clients home for dinner, so I did a good deal of entertaining. We belonged to the Briar Ridge Country Club, and he belonged to the tennis association. We both played tennis, and on weekends we enjoyed meeting with friends at the Club while the kids hung around the swimming pool or played tennis. We had a good life.

Tonight I had laundry to do and the kids' clothes to iron, so I got up and started a load of washing. I didn't mind; my life with Jim and our kids was simple and sweet, and what was most important in my life wasn't the bank. It was my family.

I was involved in the community of Briar Ridge, belonged to the Junior Women's Club with women who were heads of their own companies as well as some non-working wives and mothers, like me. We had a goal of improving our community, and I was proud that we were making a difference. We had just raised enough money to put yellow speed bumps in all the roads in town, which kept drivers from veering over the center divide.

The next morning I skipped getting coffee on the way to work because I didn't want to be late. I could get coffee at the bank. When I arrived I saw Deanna and Gerri standing together in the parking lot. Deanna had her hand on her forehead and Gerri was patting her on the back. They both looked hung-over.

This happened just about every day. Both girls were in their late twenties and apparently were looking for Mr. Right in all the wrong places. Bars, I guessed.

Deanna raised her head and looked at me as I walked by. "How is Miss Sunshine today?"

That was rude, but I decided to overlook it. "Fine," I said. "Just fine."

She glared at me. Gerri was a little overweight, and her clothes never quite fit. She overdid her makeup and painted lines around her lips and filled in with a different color. I'm sure she thought she looked beautiful except that she frowned most of the time unless, of course, a good-looking man was standing at her teller window.

Inside, Deanna brushed past me to get her money drawer from the vault, then suddenly went running for the ladies room. I just closed my eyes, shook my head, and opened my window for the first customer. I knew most of them by name, where they worked, who their children were, and even the names of their dogs. Carol told me I had a way of making each person feel like a million bucks by the time they left my window. She also said I might be ready for my own branch soon.

I couldn't help but be excited about the prospect. They had faith in me and my abilities.

Then it was mid-morning and suddenly there was Jim standing in my customer line.

"Jim! What are you doing here?"

"I came to congratulate on your new head teller position." He reached in his pocket and out came a red jewelry store box. Inside was a beautiful gold watch. "That's so you're on time for work every day," he said with a smile.

I reached my hand through my teller window and he clasped it. Our eyes locked and he mouthed "I love you." Then he blew me a kiss and said, "I'll see you tonight."

After he left the tellers just stared at me and shook their heads. "Well, Mary Poppins," Deanna said, "that's quite a nice husband you have there."

Carol smiled at me from across the room and motioned me over to her desk. I locked up my drawer and joined her. "Today I want you to help me hire three new tellers," she said.

Wow. I was excited at the prospect and flattered by her confidence in me. We interviewed them one by one. The first woman's hair was a mess and she wore jeans and flip-flops. Not exactly what we had in mind. Her math was equally awful. "Don't you have machines to add everything up?" she asked.

One of Carol's eyebrows went up. "We are looking for the right person," she said dryly. "Someone who can add and keep her money drawer balanced daily. And who dresses appropriately."

The woman glanced down at her jeans. "Could I come back?"

"That won't be necessary," Carol answered.

The next applicant was 15 minutes late, but at least she looked the part. Carol told her to take the qualification test over to the desk across the room and come back when she finished. The test was simple common sense and easy math. After an hour, the woman finally returned, and I glanced at her test. She hadn't even finished the questions. Carol told her nicely she would not be needed, and we both watched her leave.

"Gosh, they all seem rough around the edges, don't they?" I said.

Carol's other eyebrow went up. "They sure do."

The next woman came at 2 p.m. Her name was Marcia and I had a positive reaction to her right away. She was smart, pleasant, and funny. Her letters of recommendation were outstanding, and she dressed nicely. She sailed through the math test and then I watched as she counted down a drawer. She was fast and efficient.

Carol and I discussed her application and we gave her the job on the spot. "You'll start tomorrow, at nine sharp," Carol said. "Rose and I will be training you."

I was elated that Carol had asked me to help evaluate the applicants and even more elated that I would be helping to train Marcia. I went back to my window and started to help customers.

Deanna spent most of the day in the restroom, as did Gerri. Laura and I handled most of the customers all day. Laura was a jolly person in her twenties who always had a smile on her face, even when things were stressful. She was tall and she always wore understated clothes to work, nothing too flashy and just the right style for her age. Occasionally she would go to a bar with Gerri and Deanna after work, but she kept things in control, none of the wee-hour-of-the-morning stuff.

At the end of the day, Carol made an announcement. "We're going to address employee after-hours activities today after we close."

I kept looking at my new watch all day, and when closing time came, Deanna and Gerri dragged themselves over to Carol's desk and I sat down next to them.

"Ladies, we are here to work, not spend the day running to and from the restroom. I am not here to tell you what you can do in your free time, but if it affects your full day at work, as it did today, measures will be taken. Deanna and Gerri, you can consider this a warning."

Being reprimanded in front of everyone caught them both off guard, but the moment the meeting was over, both girls got up and walked toward the door, giving each other high-fives. "I'll beat you to The Brewery!" Deanna said. Gerri yelled to Laura, "Do you want to join us?"

Laura looked at Carol, then at me. "Not this time," she said.

I drove home to cook dinner and help my children with their homework. I told Jim about the two girls at work who spent the day in a drunken stupor.

He raised his eyebrows. "And they kept them on the line all day?"

"They were mostly in the restroom. It was ugly."

Jim laughed and shook his head. "You would have fired them, right?"

The next day at work I learned how to audit the bank vault. I knew how to balance the merchant window, which involved going to the front part of the vault where a specified amount of money was kept for the merchant teller. This was where I would be putting large sums of money the merchants brought in for deposit. After I learned how to audit the vault, I would have access to the second door of the vault where all loans and more currency and coins were stored.

One morning Mike, the chief bank officer, opened the door for the employees. Mike was very tall, in his mid-thirties, and he was a real stickler for accuracy. I had walked to the teller line, but no one was there to buzz me in. In fact, no one was around at all. I waited a few minutes and finally Carol arrived.

"Good morning, Rose."

"Hi, Carol. Where is everybody?"

"They're all upstairs in the boardroom. They were asked to come in early today for a meeting." The boardroom had a long table with 30 chairs around it for stockholders and board members. The president and vice-president of the bank also had their offices upstairs.

"Really? I didn't hear about this."

Carol gave me a smile. "You have a perfect teller record, so you didn't need to attend."

"Oh?" I glanced up but she didn't say anything more, so I walked into the vault to retrieve my money drawer. I was all set up when I looked up to see the other tellers emerge from the meeting. All of them were frowning. Apparently they'd been scolded about something.

"Why weren't you at the meeting?" Deanna asked.

I just shrugged. "I didn't know about the meeting." I decided not to tell her about my perfect teller record.

Deanna was tall with long, unruly hair that she tried to straighten. She wore her dresses a little too short and a little too tight, and her heels were at least five inches high. She used very red lipstick and thick mascara with black eyeliner, and when she walked she swayed her hips, I guess because she thought it was attractive. Actually, in those high heels it made her look slightly pigeon-toed.

David appeared at my elbow. "One of the board members needs to cash a large check." I said my window was open, and he sent him over to me. The man was grey-haired and grumpy, wearing a white shirt and tie with his jacket flung over his arm. He didn't look happy, and he said he needed $10,000 in cash.

I went into the vault, gave Charlene a receipt from my cash drawer to the vault, and she counted the money out to me. I put it through the money counter, then counted it again in front of the customer.

David was watching me. "I wish the other tellers would do exactly what you just did," he said. "If they did, they wouldn't come up short at the end of the day. Then he added, "Let's audit the vault."

The vault had two areas of access. The first alarm and codes were needed for the vault entrance, where safety deposit boxes were kept, along with merchant deposits and money for the tellers throughout the day. The back wall had another security alarm and required a secret pass-code for entry. This part of the vault had more coins and even more currency, all loan documentation and loan ID numbers with pertinent customer information. Two people were required to be in the vault if it was opened, a teller and a manager.

Auditing the vault usually happened every month. The bank needed to keep track of every loan, all types of loans, all currency, and any outstanding money that goes into each teller drawer. The money all had to add up, along with what was outstanding in loans. The board of directors had full disclosure; the stockholders got quarterly reports.

I closed my customer window, locked my cash drawer, and proceeded to learn how to balance the vault. This entailed counting all the coins stacked on the vault floor. Money was stacked by dollars, fives, tens, and hundreds, all wrapped in white bands. When you opened the vault, the currency, as the tellers referred to it, was right there in plain sight. Safety deposit boxes lined one wall, and the vault teller kept track of those. Only the vault teller was allowed in the vault.

Charlene and the branch manager, David, were the only employees entrusted with balancing the vault, but they needed a backup person in case someone called in sick. Charlene was a stickler for balancing to the penny. She was in her late twenties, rather plain looking with brown hair; she was raising her daughter by herself. David was short, with an abrupt manner; he always wore black suits and shirts with pointy collars and shiny black shoes. David was very responsible; he was an immigrant from the Middle East, a family man, and he was grateful to be employed by the bank.

All the tellers wore keys on swirly bracelets on their wrists; you could hear them jingle when they walked around the office. Those keys were kept in a drawer in the vault so no one could duplicate them and get into another teller's money drawer. If a key were ever left unattended, the teller would immediately be terminated.

We walked to the vault at the back of the bank. He placed his key in the vault door and within seconds the timer opened the vault. "An alarm will go off," he said. "Only you and I and the chief officer will know we are in here, aside from the security cameras that film everything."

I looked up and sure enough cameras were mounted in the four corners of the ceiling; I had never noticed them before. They were small, blended in with the wall color, and had a yellow light underneath. Cameras were also located on each door of the bank, all the windows, and any wall that had a blind side. The managers' desks as well as the teller stations were rigged with alarms.

"You can tell the cameras are working by that yellow light on the bottom," David explained.

Sure enough, that light was on.

The vault door slowly swung open, and I stood there in awe at the amount of money that was kept there. David and I finished this task, penciling in all the loans and teller drawer amounts. Each number went into a specific column, and I had to include the money in the front of the vault as well as in the back. The whole bank balanced to the penny.

"Very good, Rose," he said. "You did an excellent job, quick and precise. I liked how you counted the money twice before you reported the amount to me. You could be promoted to head vault teller if you wanted."

I was thrilled. I really worked hard to do a good job, and now I was being noticed and praised.

"One more thing," he said. "See this transaction receipt?"

"Yes." I looked at it intently. I made sure to listen to all instructions in detail. I'd always liked the idea of learning about mortgages and loans and maybe even running a small branch. If I wanted to run a branch by myself some day, I needed to learn how to do everything the correct way. All the procedures were done for the specific reason of keeping the bank running and keeping it balanced.

"Always draw a line where you have balanced, initial it, and date it. That identifies you as the one who balanced the vault, and the amounts you balance should match the starting figures for the next day."

"Got it." I drew the line and initial the receipt, and David initialed it as well.

"There," he said. "You've balanced the bank."

I felt pretty proud of myself

Chapter Three

The next morning both kids woke up on the wrong side of the bed and it was a struggle getting them into the car and off to school. Neither one of them said much on the way, so I put on my favorite radio station and turned up the volume.

"Mom, do we have to listen to that elevator music?" Anthony complained.

"Yeah," Margaret agreed.

I held my tongue, but thank goodness school was right around the corner. They walked onto the school grounds and I pulled out of the parking lot, drove to Real Caffeine, a drive-through coffee shop. Linny, the manager, always had my coffee waiting for me. What a nice gesture, I thought. I sure didn't want to be late for work.

In the bank parking lot I saw Laura and Deanna huddled together, talking about something. Deanna was very animated, and I wondered what had happened.

Inside, Carol waved hurriedly and motioned me over. "Rose, there's been a development. Claire has been . . . " She swallowed and I thought her eyes looked odd. "Well, Claire won't be at the bank any longer."

"You fired Claire? Why?"

"I can't go into that," she said hurriedly. "But you know the branch over in Westville? You'll be going over there immediately.

"Me?"

"You've picked up all the bank tasks very quickly, and I know you're ready. I'm sure you will do fine, and I am only a phone call away if you need help."

I could hardly talk, but I managed to ask, "Who will I be working with?"

"Joel is the branch manager. He can show you the ropes. You'll also be coming back to the main branch from time to time for training on procedures."

I just looked at her.

"I want you to head over there now, see what the branch is like and where things are. I'll come over later this morning."

My mind was swirling. I'm going to be working at the Westville branch! Maybe this would lead to eventually running it? I was excited at the prospect. Then I got nervous. Am I really ready to do this? Well, even if I wasn't, I would learn the ins and outs of running the bank from Joel. I got into my car and drove straight over to the Westville branch.

The building was wedged between a coffee shop and a candy store; there was a small grocery store around the corner and a beauty shop and a restaurant across the way. A cement wall wrapped around the entire small shopping mall and a few old oak trees shaded the building.

I smoothed my skirt and checked my makeup and lipstick in the mirror. I was as ready as I would ever be. I got out of the car and walked into the Westville branch.

There stood Joel. He was short and a bit stout, with grey hair and a sad-looking face, wearing grey slacks and a long-sleeved white shirt that he tugged on constantly. The smell of cigarettes clung to him, and he looked . . . well, nervous.

"Hello, Rose."

"Good morning, Joel."

He pulled on his shirt sleeve. "Want to get started?"

"Yes. I've never been here, so maybe you could show me the vault and where the ATM is located." I was nervous, too, but I tried hard not to show it.

"Let's start with the vault, since you need to open a cash drawer. We will both have teller drawers open throughout the day, but it never gets so busy that just one person can't handle things."

"That will be different from the main branch; all five tellers are busy all day long."

"Every day we'll both be balancing the branch and the money drawers, as well as the ATM. You'll also be opening some new accounts and loans."

"Sounds good." It sounded fantastic! I was so eager to get started I could hardly stand still.

Joel kept talking. He spoke very fast, and I had to concentrate to hear his words. "Rose, you will be here, right behind the locked door." He gestured at the teller's station. The restroom is right behind you, and no one but you and I can use it. If I have to call the main branch, I step into the restroom and partially close the door for privacy; you may find you need to do this also from time to time."

"I see." It was cramped quarters, but I felt I could handle anything and couldn't wait to get started.

The first day went like a breeze. I met new people and started right away to memorize faces and little things about them. I noticed that Joel opened accounts and then he left them in his desk drawer. That seemed odd, but maybe I hadn't understood the branch procedures. Before I went to close for the day, one of the main branch merchants came into the Westville branch.

"Hi, Samuel. How's everything at your store? I didn't know you used this branch."

He looked blank for a second. "Oh. Well, yes, I do. It's on my way home." He plopped a huge burlap bag of money onto the counter at my teller station. "I didn't have time to add it all up. I'm sure you will, and just put it in my account as usual."

I was flabbergasted that he had no idea how much money was in that bag. This was not good procedure, bringing in cash with no accounting of how much there was. I wondered how long Samuel had been doing this, and if he brought his deposits to the main branch the same way.

Samuel left, and I quickly counted the cash, made the deposit, and reminded myself to send the receipt to Samuel. Everything went fine from then on until the end of the day.

"Joel, I'm going to close now. Don't you have some new accounts for me to enter into the system?"

"Oh, those," he said. "We'll get to them tomorrow. Go ahead and close."

I knew that was not bank policy, and I waited for him to tell me why this was a good idea, but he didn't. When Joel stepped out in front of the office, I went over to his desk and took a peek. The cash and checks with the deposits did not add up. The cash was missing. Had Joel taken money out of Samuel's deposits?

Stunned, I tried to think rationally. I memorized the account numbers and wrote down the actual amount the deposits should have been. I also started a log. I had a hunch something was not on the up and up, and at first I tried to shrug it off.

But I found I couldn't.

Joel stepped back inside the bank as I was balancing out my money drawer, and we both went to count the ATM. I told him I could do it and suggested that he process his cash drawer, so he went back outside.

I found the ATM was $40,000 off. The back of my neck got prickly. Something was wrong here.

I had a small camera in my purse, left over from one of my daughter's biology field study projects. Thinking there was something really off here, something that I didn't want to risk getting blamed for, I took a photo of the actual numbers of the running daily transaction receipt in the ATM machine, and then I took another photo of my balancing sheet.

Something about this didn't make sense. I began wondering why Claire was no longer working here at the branch; I knew Carol said she had been fired, and now I wondered if she was part of the problem here. Or maybe Claire had been part of it?

And then out of the blue came an awful thought: *Had Claire been . . . ?*

The next thing I had to do was balance the vault. To my horror, the vault did not balance; it was $60,000 short! I went over every step, re-counting the money, picking up the figures from the day before. I got my camera back out, took a photo of both my work calculations and the vault balancing transaction sheets for the past week.

I started to shake. There was a huge problem here. I needed to get someone over to the Westville branch to see this. Now.

Chapter Four

Joel walked in after his cigarette break. "Time to close up." He locked the front door and, since I'd just finished balancing it, I was locking up the vault. He stood in the middle of the floor, pulling at his shirt sleeves. Something about it gave me the jitters.

"Well," he said at last, "it was a good day. I'll see you tomorrow."

I looked right at him. "I'll lock up after myself and see you in the morning." I was a bundle of nerves. I got in my car and just sat there. How could he say it had been a good day? What was he thinking? How could we leave the bank knowing it was $100,000 short?

Suddenly I knew what I had to do. I drove straight over to the main branch. Please, please let someone still be there. I ran to the front door and knocked on the window.

"We're closed," someone said from inside.

"No, please. I work here. Please let me in."

Carol unlocked the door. "Rose! What are you doing here?

"Carol," I gasped. "Something's wrong."

She gave me a quick, sharp look. What? How did your day go?"

I studied her face. Could I tell her? I hesitated so long she reached out and touched my arm. "Rose?"

"Um, I think the Westville branch is, uh, not run very tightly."

She frowned. "What do you mean?"

"Well, at the end of the day I couldn't get the vault to balance. Or the ATM, either."

Both her eyebrows went up. "Did you find the mistakes?"

"Yes. And Joel acted like there was nothing wrong." I told her the amounts. "Protocol says that when you have large losses like that, you call for a supervisor."

"Are you going to talk to Fredric?"

"Yes, that's why I came over."

"He's in his office, upstairs." I went upstairs and knocked on his door.

"Come in," I heard from his office.

The president, Fredric, was in early sixties, short and fat; he always wore very loud ties. He acted like he was a powerful man who didn't care what he looked like. He'd taken over three other banks in the past 10 years and turned them around. He had four ex-wives, and the rumor was that he was looking for wife number five. He was abrupt and acted as if he knew it all, and if there was a disagreement about anything, it was his way or the highway.

He came toward me and purposely touched my arm, then left his hand there. I flinched.

"Fredric, I just started to work at the Westville branch, and something there is not right."

"Sit down, Rose. What do you mean, something is not right?"

"For one thing, nothing balances."

"Are you sure?"

"Yes," I said. "I am sure. I re-counted everything to double-check."

"Well, don't worry about it. I'll get right on it. But," he added, again touching my arm, "you need to be quiet about this."

"Of course. Though I just told Carol about the losses."

He gave me a long look. "Okay, now tell me exactly what you saw."

I told him that the ATM machine was $40,000 off, and that the vault was off by $60,000. Then I told him about the new accounts that were still in Joel's desk drawer and that I'd noticed the cash from Samuel's deposit was missing.

"Those are very big accusations," Fredric growled.

"But that's exactly what I saw. What should I do about it?"

"Nothing for now. I'll take care of it."

"It's kind of funny," I added, "but Joel said something odd. Before we closed he said 'this was a good day.' But I know it couldn't have been a good day, and I wondered what he meant by that."

I got up to leave Fredric's office, and when he put his hand out to shake mine I noticed something. It was cold and clammy. I looked down at his sweaty hand gripping mine and instantly broke contact. Something just didn't feel right. I looked up at his face and saw something that unnerved me.

He looked angry. Was he angry at the situation? Or at me? Hurriedly I left his office, shutting the door behind me, and then I hesitated in the hallway with my back to the door. As I stood there I heard Fredric's voice on the phone.

"Joel, why did you ask for Rose? It's only her first day at the branch and she's on to you. We need to get her the hell out of there. And to make matters worse, now Carol is involved."

I couldn't breathe. I couldn't believe what I'd heard. Quickly I walked down the hallway and down the stairs; I almost ran past Carol, but she put out her hand and stopped me.

"What did Fredric say?"

I thought frantically. What should I say? "He says there is an explanation and for me not to worry about it." I didn't tell her he had immediately telephoned Joel or what I'd overheard.

"Those losses must be just errors in addition," Carol said. I said I agreed, but I couldn't wait to get out the door.

Outside I took a deep breath and rushed to my car. I had to do what was right, but I wondered if I had the nerve. My hands shook so violently I could hardly start the engine.

The Briar Ridge police station was downtown. I drove by it almost every day, but today I needed to talk to someone about what I suspected. I had to find a place to park, which was never easy on First Street. I found a space at another bank down the street from the police station.

I knew a lot of police officers' children because of my own kids' school activities, but today I didn't want to run into any of them. I had seen something that was just plain wrong, even though I couldn't quite put my finger on what it was, and I knew I needed to tell the police about it.

My palms were wet and my hands trembled. I walked up the steps to the front desk and asked the first person I saw, "Who do I talk to if I think I saw something that is against the law?"

The officer stared at me. "You need to speak to an officer in investigative work. Let me get someone from that office on the phone for you."

I was immediately sent upstairs to see "Tony." I stepped into the elevator and glanced at my watch. It was close to 6:30 p.m. Jim would not be happy about my being so late. What was I going to tell him?

I walked into a hallway and all the way to the end. People were all over the place on the telephone, with stacks of paperwork on their desks. I found Antonio Alverazo's office and stood in the doorway.

"Hello," came a voice from behind a cupboard. "I'm Tony. Come on in."

"I'm Rose Ryan."

He stepped into his office. "What can I help you with?" Tony was tall and had a Spanish accent. I noticed his shirt tail wasn't tucked in and he had a pencil behind his left ear and a small notebook with pens in his shirt pocket. His desk was cluttered with papers and files; boxes filled with more files were stacked up on the floor in the corner.

I started to sweat. Tony noticed my uneasiness. "Have a seat," he said.

I sat down.

"Okay, now tell me what brings you here today."

I gulped in a huge breath of air. Could I really do this? "I work at a bank," I began. "The Westville branch of Harvest Bank. And I think something wrong is happening there."

I had his attention. "Like what?" he said sharply.

"I'm new at this branch. Today was my first day. Nothing at the bank would balance when we closed, and the manager kept new account transactions in his desk drawer, which is against bank protocol." I went on to tell him about the vault and ATM machine shortages.

He sat up in his chair. "How long have you worked at Harvest Bank?"

"Over two years."

"Has anything like this happened before?"

"Not that I know of."

"Do you have a good teller record?"

"Yes, I do. I'm the head teller, and they've been showing me how to manage different areas of the bank."

"What else can you tell me about today at the Westville branch? Tell me everything and name every person you think might be involved."

"Can we at least close your door?" I asked.

"It's not necessary. Everything is being taped and put on film."

I began to shake.

"What's wrong?" he asked.

"I am implicating the president of this bank along with the Westville branch manager!"

"Oh, I see," Tony said. He was on the edge of his chair by now, and he

20

looked me in the eye. "I need to call in the FBI."

My mouth dropped open. "Oh my God." I grabbed my purse and started to stand up. "I'll lose my job."

"Rose, sit down. You may be in danger. You need to be very careful until the FBI contacts you, and that will be very soon. I'll put an undercover officer on your tail, and you'll also have security coverage at home. And we'll have to monitor your family. This isn't something we take lightly, and you shouldn't, either."

"But-- "

"Don't say anything to anyone, not even your husband. The less anyone else knows, the better."

"I can't tell my husband?"

Tony shook his head, and it began to sink in. I was going to be followed. "Why will I be followed?" I blurted.

"For your own safety." I looked at him, shaking my head. Was this the right thing to do? Then I told him I'd mentioned the matter to my supervisor at the main branch.

"What is her full name and what position does she hold at the bank?"

I told him.

"What exactly did you tell her?"

"That I thought something was wrong at the Westville branch."

"Don't talk to anyone about this."

"How in the world will I be able to do that? I have a job at this bank."

"Just don't talk about it," he said. "And be vague when you tell your husband about your day."

He looked at me and smiled not very convincingly. "We will have more to tell you in time, and you will have more to tell the authorities when they contact you. Now, what is your car make and model and your license plate number? I'll run your plates to make sure we're following you 24-7."

I would be followed? My family would be followed? *There is more to this, but he's not telling me.*

"Oh my God, this is going to change my life." I began to regret going to the police.

"Don't worry, Mrs. Ryan," Tony said. "You won't even know we're around. That's all the information I need from you right you. You'll get a call tonight."

I got up to leave. I looked around the office and noticed papers and boxes everywhere but no photos of Tony or his wife or children. He noticed what I noticed. "People are crazy to put their personal lives out there."

Right then I decided I would take down my family photos at work. And now my family was going to be watched by law enforcement. *What have I done?*

I walked slowly to my car, looking at everything around me, the buildings, the bushes, the trees, the sidewalk. Nothing looked different, but everything sure felt different. I climbed into my car and drove home, watching in my rearview mirror for a car following me.

How in the world could I not tell Jim? I had horrible doubts about this whole business.

Did I do the right thing? I was scared to death.

"Wow," Jim said when I got home. "You're really late."

I rushed over and hugged him, and I couldn't help but hold onto him. Finally I let go and said quickly, "What a day at work!"

He shook his head. "I know how that can happen. Did you balance?"

I wanted to scream, *That's not it at all, Jim!* The bank was off a lot of money and I went to the police and now they're calling in the FBI. I might be in danger. You and the kids might be in danger. And oh, by the way, we are all going to be followed by the Briar Ridge police.

Instead I said calmly, "We are short three tellers at the main branch, so they sent me to the Westville branch to help the manager there."

"Those things happen with work," Jim said.

I changed the subject and asked how everyone's day had gone. The kids had things going on in school and homework due, so they were eating on the go tonight. Jim and I watched them take their plates to the other room to study while they ate.

Just then the phone rang. I popped up quickly to answer it before anyone else had a chance.

"Is this Rose Ryan?"

"Yes."

"This is FBI agent Scott Aiden. I will meet you tomorrow morning at 6:30 at a place called Sweet Treat Bakery. I know what you look like, so I will approach you."

Chapter Five

The next morning I thought about all the reasons I shouldn't get involved in this mess. But then I had to remind myself that I was already involved. Today I would find out to what degree.

I kissed Jim goodbye and told him not to forget to pick up the kids from school. Then I drove down First Street to Main and turned right. Sweet Treat Bakery was about a mile or so farther, on the corner. When I turned into the parking lot I noticed it was packed with cars, and that meant the bakery would be crowded. With all these people, how would I identify this FBI person?

I walked in through the glass doors, went to the customer line, and stood there. A woman came up behind me and touched my arm. "Come over here."

I began to perspire. Oh, God, what had I gotten myself into?

She was ordinary looking. She walked me to a table and said her name was Sara. I sat down across from a clean-cut looking man. "We flew in from Washington overnight," she said.

He showed me his credentials, and then she showed me hers. By this time my legs were shaking so hard the table shook. They ordered some coffee for me, but I couldn't hold my cup without sloshing it all over the place, so I grabbed both my hands and held them in my lap.

Briefly I told them about my day at the Westville branch and how nothing had balanced and that it was $100,000 short. I also told them what had happened with Fredric, the bank president, and what I had overheard him tell Joel. Sara kept an eye on the people in the coffee shop while Scott took notes in a memo book.

"Rose, you did the right thing," he said. "Your suspicion brought you to us, and now we'll try to get to the bottom of this."

"But . . . I'm not sure I can keep this to myself." I felt like my nerves were about ready to unravel.

"We can't stress enough that this is a top secret matter. You cannot talk about this to anyone, and that includes your husband and your family. It's possible you're working with dangerous people."

Oh, my God, how in the world am I supposed to deal with dangerous people? "How am I going to keep this from my husband?" My voice cracked. "What if I accidentally say something to someone?" I was losing my nerve.

"By the end of the day, Sara and I will both be working at the bank, in different departments."

My jaw dropped.

"After our work schedules are in place, we'll set up our next meeting with you. In the meantime, Rose, remember you're being watched everywhere you go, especially at the bank. Find out as much as you can without bringing attention to yourself and keep track of everything. We need to compile evidence. We're not positive, but it's usually more than one person involved in bank schemes."

Bank schemes, I repeated to myself. I covered my mouth in shock. How could he be so matter of fact?

"Now," Scott continued, "you need to get to work. Just act like nothing is wrong and observe everything you can. We'll be in touch with you."

Sara leaned forward. "The next time you see us, we'll be working within the bank. But if something comes up, here's a phone number you can call, day or night. Keep it with you. It might be smart to memorize it."

I took the slip of paper she handed me, walked out of the bakery, and didn't stop shaking until I reached my car. I didn't even look back to see if they followed me outside. I got into my car and slid into the driver's seat. *What had just happened here?*

What had happened? I almost laughed out loud, but instead I brought my hand on my forehead and shook my head. I'd just had breakfast with the FBI!

I drove back to the Westville branch and turned into the parking lot, and there was Joel, standing by his car smoking a cigarette. I got out of my car and walked up to the front door. Joel came over, trying to look as if everything was perfectly normal. We punched in the security code and waited for the alarm to go silent so we could enter; I started for the vault when I heard Joel's voice.

"How are you this morning, Rose?"

"Fine. I'm fine. How about you?"

"Good. Will you please open the vault while I go get coffee?"

"Sure."

He walked out of the bank, leaving me alone with the front door unlocked. That wasn't proper procedure! Someone could just walk in before I was set up.

I was still shaking from my breakfast meeting with Scott and Sara when I looked up to see a man walk into the bank. He had tattoos all over his arms, lightning bolts on one and a skull on the other, and a cigarette dangled between his lips.

"I'm sorry," I said, "you aren't allowed to smoke in here."

"Is that right?" He didn't take the cigarette out of his mouth.

"Yes, it is."

"Where's Joel?"

"He's next door, getting coffee."

He walked out, flicking cigarette ashes on the carpet. I sure hoped the security cameras got a photo of him! I looked up at the cameras, but the yellow light wasn't on. Oh, no, it wasn't working! Had someone deliberately turned it off?

I remembered the phone number Sara had given me, still in my skirt pocket, so I went to the phone on the nearest desk and dialed the number.

"The security cameras are off," I said.

"Okay," Scott said in my ear. "I'm on it."

Joel returned and introduced the tattooed man as his brother, but he didn't give his name.

"Joel," I said, "we need to finish our business so we can open."

"Oh, Rose, go ahead and open up. I'll be right out front with my brother."

Things were more than lax at this branch. *Joel sure sets his own rules.* I locked my money drawer and walked over to the ATM machine and opened it, then went to the vault to fill up the ATM machine. All this time I hoped no customers would come in because no one was on duty.

I saw Joel walk back in and quickly go to his desk and pick up some papers. And then I saw that something had slid in between the pages. It looked like green cash. I tried not to look at it too intently and closed the

ATM machine as fast as I could. When I looked up, there was a customer at my window.

"Hello," I said to the elderly woman. "How are you this morning?"

"Great, sweetie. I'm here to close out my T-bill account."

"Do you have your account number?"

"Right here." She handed me the small bank book with the number and her name on the first page, and I punched the number into my bank computer. And there it was: a $100,000

T-bill account flashed onto my computer screen.

With a zero balance!

My heart started to pound. "Mrs. O'Brien, can you tell me when you opened this account?"

"Yes, it was the week my husband died. It was his life insurance money."

"And you haven't touched this since then, is that right?"

"Never. But now I'm moving out of state to be closer to my daughter in Mississippi, and I need the money."

Oh, God, what should I do? "I'm sure your daughter will enjoy having you close by," I managed.

"I'm very sad to leave my house," she said slowly. "My husband and I owned it for fifty years."

This was just awful! Her money was gone. I told her I needed an officer's approval from the main branch and excused myself; then I picked up the phone and stepped into the restroom. I closed the door and dialed.

The connection seemed to ring forever . . . one ring, two rings. Scott picked up on the third ring. "Scott," I whispered. "Help. A hundred thousand dollars has disappeared. The account number is valid."

I gave it to him, and in a moment he said, "I have it. I'm at the main branch. Give her a cashier's check for the full amount and I'll call you back later and tell you how to offset the transaction. Put it aside, not in the work that will go to the proofing department."

Trembling, I hung up and walked back to Mrs. O'Brien. "Is everything okay?" she asked.

"Yes," I said as calmly as I could. "Mrs. O'Brien, who should I make the cashier's check out to?"

"Mrs. Tamara O'Brien. My daughter will put it in her account until I decide what to do with the money."

My hands shook. Joel was still standing out front, smoking with his brother. The phone rang. "Rose, it's Scott here. We're working on the security cameras and I'm sending Sara over to help out."

At that moment Joel walked back into the bank. "Joel's here," I murmured into the receiver."

"Right. Don't do anything to perturb him until Sara gets there. She's on her way."

I decided to keep Mrs. O'Brien with me until Sara arrived. "Mrs. O'Brien, have a seat right over here while I make out your cashier's check. And let me get you a cup of coffee."

"Oh, thank you, my dear."

I was stalling and Joel was watching, pacing back and forth in front of me. Just then a woman in a very nice blue suit walked in. Sara! I could have kissed her.

"Who do I talk to about opening an account?" Sara inquired.

"I can help you as soon as I finish with my customer here." My hands were so twitchy I knew Joel would notice. When I finished typing the cashier's check, Mrs. O'Brien came over to my window and I had her sign it. I gave her an account book with her T-bill number on it, marked Closed.

Sara noticed my unease. She leaned forward and intoned, "Security is on its way to fix the cameras. Give me that transaction you just worked on."

"I think Joel dismantled the security system," I murmured.

"Yes," she replied in a steady voice. "That is exactly the type of account I want to open."

Just then Joel reappeared. "Can I help, Rose?"

I steadied my voice. "Should I work the teller window or open this new CD account?" I asked.

"Joel looked at Sara. "I'll open this account."

I watched in awe as Sara took $20,000 in cash out of her purse to open a CD. Then Security from the main office came in and announced that they'd noticed the system was down. I let Joel do the talking.

"I didn't call you," he said.

"The main branch sent us to make sure everything was working."

Joel kept frowning, but I was relieved. Sara opened four CDs, totaling $80,000. The Security guy stayed most of the day trying to fix the camera he said wasn't working. In fact, he announced, none of the cameras were working.

A few minutes later Sara came to my teller window, and I slid the $100,000 transaction to her. She stuffed it in her purse and left.

The rest of the day was uneventful until it came time to balance at the end of the day. Sara's $20,000 in cash had disappeared. Only her checks totaling $60,000 for the CD were with the paperwork.

At a quarter to five, Joel's brother returned and announced that he wanted the forms to read over for a new account. He was unshaven and his hair was uncombed. As Joel handed the pages to him, I noticed something stuffed in between the forms; I was positive it was the missing $20,000.

At 5 o'clock, Carol from the main branch arrived unexpectedly and locked the front door behind her. "Rose, how was your day here?"

I smiled and glanced at Joel. "It was a good day for the branch office. A lot of CDs were opened."

Carol turned to Joel. "Joel, you can go on over to the main office for that meeting you're attending. Rose, you will be closing up today. Here's your key. Don't keep it with your personal keys, in case you lose them. I'll stay today to make sure you close correctly."

I balanced the ATM and the vault while Carol watched. Then I balanced my teller drawer and announced that we were $20,000 short.

"It looks like it was cash, too," Carol said.

I stepped in close to her. "Look in Joel's desk drawer," I whispered. She slid it open and sure enough, there was $20,000 in cash.

She sent me a quizzical look. "What is this doing in his drawer?" I wondered what it was he had handed to his brother, but I was relieved the money was here.

Carol took out a folder and wrote something in it. "We're done here. Let's lock up and go home."

I stopped at the grocery store and got home just as Jim and the kids were arriving. I hugged Jim hard and held him a bit longer than usual. I even hugged Anthony as he walked by. I felt safe at home.

"How was everyone's day?" I heard a few groans about the homework load, and I just smiled.

Jim turned on the TV news and settled in his favorite chair with the newspaper. I had just put the potatoes in the oven when the news broadcaster's voice sliced into my consciousness.

"A fisherman reported finding the body of a young woman on the wharf close to midnight last night. She had been shot. A witness reported seeing two men leaving the scene, but so far no arrests have been made. The body has not yet been identified."

The news made me queasy, and then it got worse. Jim lowered the newspaper.

"Listen to this, Rose. Police suspect the death of a young woman found shot last night is connected with a disgruntled boyfriend involved with drugs. Says here they found a large quantity of drugs stashed at the water's edge of the wharf. Isn't that where the kids like to fish?"

"Well, not anymore," I called from the kitchen. "Sometimes I wonder what our little town is coming to."

That night my stomach was more than queasy.

Chapter Six

I couldn't sleep. Jim was busy with his new company and didn't notice anything was amiss with me, and I was grateful that no questions were asked so I didn't have to think up any lies.

I lay awake watching the clock, trying not to think about the FBI. I did have a nightmare that woke me up, and I moved closer to Jim to hug him and tried to go back to sleep. I kept telling myself I was safe now.

Two days later Scott and Sara called an emergency meeting at Sweet Treat Bakery. "Rose, we need you to start compiling a paper trail. Be discreet and use some magazines to store copies of the paperwork to hand over to us. We're afraid more people are involved, maybe some of the tellers at the main branch."

"Oh my Lord, who?"

"We're not sure yet. What we do know is that we've seen what you've seen. Joel is giving his brother money and checks from new accounts; sometimes those accounts are intercepted by you, but when you're on your lunch hour, he pockets it all. Your presence has changed what he's been doing for the past two years."

"How is it that I have noticed this but no one else at the bank has?"

Neither of them answered. Finally Scott said, "More than likely he is making sure the transactions are going through to real account numbers, but we still don't know who is involved. People could be covering for each other."

I just looked at him.

"We want you to know that when the police came in to get the security camera up and running they also installed bugs so they can monitor conversations."

"That was a policeman fixing the cameras? And . . . " I gulped. " . . . All my conversations are being monitored? I'm being taped? How can I act natural knowing I'm being taped?"

Sara patted my shaking hands across the table. "You're doing just fine, Rose."

I tried to pull myself together.

"I have already started to look into some of the accounts," I announced. "I've traced that one-hundred thousand dollar CD back to the first week Joel started working at the bank. Here's the account number. That's the account the money actually went into." I handed them the paperwork I'd copied. "I also made a photocopy of Joel's first few months of bank statements."

Scott started to smile.

"They look fishy," I continued. "Look at all the big deposits on this statement. I checked to see where the deposit money came from, and only one deposit is for his payroll. Some of the other deposits came from a loan that was opened the same date of his deposit, and some of the deposits came from new customer accounts. I can only check the computer when Joel isn't pacing around in front of my teller station. I can't go into all the loans from the Westville branch, but I think it's worth it for you to look into them to make sure nothing fishy is going on with the loans generated here at the Westville branch. You may want to check these two accounts."

I passed them the numbers. "I also think Kallie, one of the senior loan officers at the main branch, and Fredric, the bank president, are having an affair. I saw them last weekend in Griffith, holding hands and kissing."

Sara and Scott looked at me in surprise. "Good work!" Scott said. "You should come work for us if you ever want another job." Then he added, "We'll check up on Kallie and the loans she generates. We need to see what kind of money goes missing."

"Oh. Okay."

They looked at each other. "Keep up the good work, Rose. Remember, anything that doesn't seem right is usually *not* right."

The next week flew by. I found 50 more accounts that had zero balances, and the customers were apparently unaware anything was wrong. I was surprised at the number of people who didn't check their bank statements; it should say zero right on them. Then I wondered if the statements themselves had been tampered with. I called over to the main branch and asked for some printouts.

Studying one of the statements I found that Joel's ID number had been entered to change the existing account statement. I wrote the account number in my daily log, and then I called Sara and Scott to find out how I could get access to some of the earlier statements. Sara told me to just concentrate on what I could do from the Westville branch; they would take over the bank statement problem. That was a huge relief.

That night my mind raced. How many people were in on this? Did Claire's disappearance have anything to do with it? I couldn't help wondering why she was no longer at work, and why Carol seemed reluctant to talk about it.

At work each day my log grew. I was amazed at the number of accounts that had been tampered with, and I concentrated on those that had been opened with large sums of money and showed a withdrawal on the same day, by hand with no teller ID. I also started to track where all that money was going, or whether it was just going out the door with people like Joel's brother. I had a hunch, but I couldn't find out anything from Joel; he was close-mouthed.

One day his brother came into the branch. I looked up at the security cameras to make sure they were on; I wanted them to get a close-up photo of this guy. I'd never heard his name; maybe today I could find out what it was.

"Hello," I said.

"Hi, there. Where's Joel?"

"At the main branch." Joel's brother always made me nervous. He usually looked unkempt and he smoked incessantly, even though I continually advised him it was not allowed in the bank. The man had a real attitude problem. Today he was dressed in a nice shirt and slacks.

"How long will he be there?"

"He should be back soon."

A nice-looking woman walked in and accidentally closed the door on him as he was leaving. Joel's brother spun around and gave her a once-over, smiling the whole time.

"Sorry, sir," she said.

"Just call me Miles." He stood looking at her until she finished her deposit. When she turned to leave he was right behind her.

Miles, huh? I wrote his name in my log for Sara and Scott. Half an hour later, Joel returned from the main office, looking very distressed.

"Rose, have you been busy?"

"Yes. I opened three CD accounts and one T-bill and four new checking accounts. I processed them all."

He narrowed his eyes. I knew he would like to have seen the amounts and stash them in his desk drawer. "That's great, Rose. You're getting to be a good bank officer. Looks like you could run this branch without me."

I could tell he was upset. Joel was a bit strange, really. He never took vacations and often came into work sick. I figured that way he could always make sure the transactions he tried to put through to his accounts would be processed and not looked at by anyone but him.

There was something else about him, too: he was always scratching at his long shirt sleeves. Once he half-rolled up one sleeve and I saw open sores all over his arm. Sometimes when he scratched, they bled through his shirt. I didn't want to touch anything he touched. And I was grateful that the main branch kept calling meetings that were mandatory for him to attend.

Joel flung his jacket on the back of his chair, and that's when I saw the barrel of a gun poking out of his jacket pocket.

Oh my God, he had a gun! I needed to tell Scott and Sara right away. I tried to stay calm. "Oh, darn, here's that last T-bill for ten thousand dollars. Could you process this?"

He took it out of my hand and walked over to his desk. "See, you didn't get all the work done, now did you?"

I kept hoping someone would come into the bank so I wouldn't be here alone with him. And just at that moment, to my horror my son walked through the door. A cold chill went up my spine. *No! No! Don't come in!*

The phone rang and Joel answered it; he started to explain something about checking accounts to someone and I turned to Anthony. "Hello, there," I said. I was careful not to say his name. "What's up?"

"I need that check from you for that book I told you about, you know, for my school project."

Joel continued talking loudly on the phone and I prayed that he hadn't noticed my son. Hurriedly I gave him the check and he left the bank unnoticed. Joel was still on the phone, thank God. I couldn't imagine how I was going to manage occasional visits from Jim or my kids, but the sight of the gun in Joel's jacket pocket told me it was dangerous for them to be here. I glanced up at the security cameras just for reassurance.

The line at my teller window grew longer, and Joel put on his jacket and opened up his money drawer to help me. But my Lord, I was freaked out that the man standing next to me had a gun in his pocket! Five o'clock couldn't come soon enough.

Later that afternoon, Joel's brother came back and the two of them went out front to smoke. The minute they were out of sight, I dialed Scott.

"Joel has a gun!"

"I thought he might have," Scott said in a calm voice. "We have undercover officers in the vicinity, Rose. They can see you and we can hear you. We can be inside the branch in seconds."

I was losing it. "Is that supposed to make me feel better?"

Joel walked back in and I bit the inside of my cheek to keep from screaming and pretended to be talking to a customer. "You only get interest on a money market checking account," I said, trying to sound normal.

On the other end of the line, Scott said, "I understand. Hang in there, Rose."

I hung up and couldn't help looking out the front window, wondering if someone was lurking outside, staring at me. Maybe someone with a gun. Thank goodness it was Friday; I would need a long, relaxing weekend to get my nerves under control.

Thirty minutes before closing, Samuel, the store merchant, came in with another big burlap bag of money. "Hi, Rose."

"Hello. What can I do for you?"

"Here's my deposit." He plunked his bag onto the counter. "There's a blank deposit slip inside."

We need to change this protocol, I thought. Anyone could take money out of his bag and he would never know. I wondered again if Joel had already thought of just that.

Chapter Seven

Jim began telling me I was looking stressed out. "You need to just take things as they come," he advised. "Don't worry about all the rest."

But my dear husband had no idea what "*all the rest*" was. I longed to tell him what was really going on and how frightened I was, but I knew that under no circumstances could I involve him or the kids. I was caught in the middle.

And I was really beginning to worry. The kids were busy with school work and their after-school activities and had no clue that anything was wrong, but the situation ate at me. If Jim found out about any of it—the shortages at the bank, the people following us, Joel's gun, he would probably move us out of town. Scott and Sara made sure I understood that if Jim tried to interfere, he would be in danger. We would *all* be in danger.

This became a constant struggle for me. Every night, every weekend, I continued to keep quiet, hoping the problem would be solved soon.

The next day was Saturday and I could sleep in. I was exhausted all the time now, and my stomach never stopped churning from the tension at the bank. I told myself to calm down when my anxiety threatened to get away from me, but it was hard. And tonight Jim and I were entertaining two couples for dinner.

We went out for business dinners at least once a week, and I always had to make small talk during the evening. Jim counted on me to remember everyone's name and where they were from and to make them feel comfortable enough to come out and visit us again during business negotiations. We were a good team.

Sunday morning Scott called and asked me to meet him and Sara at

Sweet Treat Bakery. At the restaurant I dug in my huge black purse to retrieve the notes I'd taken.

"Kallie and Fredric are definitely an item," Sara announced. "I walked into the vault one day and there they were, locked in a clinch."

"How did they get access to the vault without Charlene?" I asked.

"I don't know, but the bank needs to work out stricter rules. Charlene was nowhere in sight."

"Rose," Scott added. "There's been a new development. We're finding discrepancies in the loan department. I'm looking into this right now, and we need to find out if they were loans from only your branch."

I looked at them. "I have a hunch Joel has figured out every possible way money could be secretly removed from customer accounts. The loans are an easy target, especially if Joel opened the account. I've already found a few loan accounts from the Westville branch that ended up with zero balances, and the customers are receiving statements that show their money is still there."

I took a deep breath. "So, we not only need to find out where the loan originated, we need to find out if it's still open and whether or not the customer is receiving statements that reflect an accurate balance. Then we need to figure out if the money went into one of the accounts we've found Joel has set up for his own gain."

"This will take some time to unravel," Scott said. I felt relieved that Sara and Scott were trying to figure this out, and as far as I was concerned, the sooner the better.

"We have people watching Joel constantly. We know he carries a gun. We have people watching your branch all the time, and they're trained to protect you. We're also keeping an eye on Joel's brother; apparently he lives right around the corner from the bank. The amount of money taken so far is staggering."

I listened closely to everything Sara and Scott were saying, but his assurance that I was protected didn't make me feel better. Inside I was a nervous wreck.

"We won't be going into much detail on the loans unless they have something to do directly with any that you and Joel have opened," Scott explained. "That way, you will know as little as possible."

"Gee, I wish I *didn't* know what I know. This web of dishonesty is really unsettling."

"You'll be going to the main branch for a few days," Sara said. "To train for making loan transactions. And one more thing--Carol is aware of us. She's a safe person and you can trust her. But don't talk about any of this within earshot of anyone else, especially bank employees. No one is on to us at this point, and we need to keep it that way."

When I got home, Jim was still sound asleep and the kids were just waking up. How many trips like this could I make before someone in my family caught on?

By Sunday night I was hurrying around the house cleaning and finishing the laundry, making sure Jim's suits were hanging along with fresh shirts and ties, and arranging my clothes for the week. At bedtime I found myself dreading what was in store for me at the bank the next day. I kept telling myself that I was doing something worthwhile, but I was really worried the whole thing would blow up on me. And on my family.

I was just opening the Westville branch when the phone rang. It was Carol. "Rose, you need to come over to the main branch today and learn about loans. I'll send Laura over to relieve you."

When Laura walked in the door I was waiting on a customer and Joel was out front, smoking. I buzzed her into the teller area, and she started to balance her money drawer. "How are you doing, Rose?"

"Fine, Laura. Thanks for coming over." I was definitely *not* fine.

I drove to the main branch, not sure what to expect. When I arrived I went directly to Carol's desk. "I have a job for you to learn," she said. "I need you to go to the loan department and double-check the amounts on the paperwork against the actual amounts shown on the bank computer. Keep the list and bring it to me at the end of the day. And Rose, don't talk to anyone else about what you find, or whether you think it's right or wrong. Just bring the list to me."

I was nervous. My stomach was really upset today and I could barely think straight.

Deanna spied me walking through the teller station. "Look," she said loudly. "It's Mary Poppins! Why are you here?"

"How are you, Deanna?" I moved past her.

"You missed a couple of great nights out," she called after me. I kept walking to the back of the loan department, where Charlene noticed me.

"Hi, Rose. Gosh, I miss you here at the main branch."

I just smiled. "I am liking the challenge at the Westville branch." *Boy, that was a complete lie!*

The loan department consisted of many people, including Val, who always talked about staying home and having children some day. There were days when I wished I'd just stayed home with my children, but I couldn't tell her that.

Val was tall and smart and always smiling. She knew all the ins and outs of loans. But when I reached the loan department, Val wasn't there. I waited a few minutes and saw the stack of loans Carol had mentioned, so I went ahead and started looking at them. Within a few minutes Val came in with Fredric; they were laughing and walking close enough to touch each other. Was something going on between them?

I was so immersed in counting up the loan amounts that I completely lost track of time until Carol came up behind me. "It's time for lunch. You want to join me?"

We went to Sweet Treat Bakery, where I was really surprised to see Scott and Sara. They waved us over to their table. "Carol, Rose, have a seat."

"How is the loan department going?" Sara asked.

"There's a lot for me to learn," I said. Then I asked about the transactions that seemed to make their way into Joel's desk drawer.

Carol shook her head. "That's been going on for two years now."

"But how can you stop that behavior?"

"Fredric has Joel's ID number on many of those loan transactions," Sara said. "Joel doesn't deposit any cash on the new accounts, and some of the checks are missing. Deanna seems to have her ID number on over-the-counter transactions that appear to have been altered. But that doesn't mean she is involved. Yet."

"Oh my gosh, that means Fredric, Joel and Deanna are all involved with this whole mess? How would they all know which transactions to tamper with?"

Carol opened her mouth, but I couldn't stop talking. "Is Joel the ringleader here? Or Fredric?"

Scott and Sara and Carol stared at me. I could see they were all thinking the same thing, but no one was saying anything out loud until Scott spoke up. "Whoa, Rose. Let's all just do the jobs at hand and try not to speculate on who's doing what, at least not yet. We're still gathering evidence."

I shook my head. I wasn't dumb; I could see things that seemed perfectly clear to me, but were they really? The more I thought about it, the bigger the group that was involved grew. Finally I couldn't keep quiet any longer.

"Hey, you guys, is anyone worried that they *all* might be carrying guns at the main branch, too?"

Sara sighed. Scott's expression was pensive, and Carol looked as nervous as I was. The subject was changed.

"We also need to get into the proof department," Sara said. "We're looking into when exactly and who exactly is physically changing the paperwork. It will be a long process."

"Is everyone balancing at the main branch?" I asked. "Or is it just the Westville branch that's off? I only noticed the discrepancies when I went to the Westville branch."

"Remember," Carol said, "the Westville branch work is picked up by Ray, our courier, at noon and 5 o'clock every day. He drives it to the main office."

"All that work goes straight to the proof department, right? Does Ray just give it to one of the tellers?"

"That work goes straight to Deanna's window," Carol replied. "Deanna takes it to the proof department. Ray stays on the customer side."

"We need to change that," Scott inserted. "Ray needs to give the work directly to the proof department."

"Have any of you noticed whether Deanna's transactions, the ones that were changed, were done when she filled in at the Westville branch?"

Sara and Scott looked like a light bulb had gone off in their brains.

"Yes," Carol said immediately. "Let's look at the dates. I'll get the calendar and trace who was at which branch when the shortages occurred. We need to look closely at each loan Joel has opened."

"Joel is careless," I said. "Let's make sure we have dates, accurate amounts, and transaction origins. I think that's the key."

After that conversation, I had no appetite for lunch.

Driving home that night I thought about the money and the paper trail that was somehow being altered and wondered when, exactly, that was being done. Ray, the courier, was in his mid-sixties. He was a really nice guy who had an equally nice wife. They couldn't afford to retire just yet, so he'd taken the job at the bank where he brought us the money from the main branch vault once or twice a week, depending on how busy we were at the Westville branch.

The money was always carried in a burlap bag, tied with a string. Ray certainly had an opportunity to open it, but then when the bag was set in the bottom of the branch vault for Joel to count, Joel would have complete access to the money straight from the bag!

The tellers' work was picked up twice a day and also placed in burlap bags. I couldn't help wondering why security in handling the money was so lax. The paperwork was just as important. If anything happened to Ray during one of his courier runs, all that work would be completely lost. Who would know what transaction to take money from?

That night Jim and I had to go out for dinner to entertain business clients, which meant I had to make dinner for the kids before we left. Jim got home late and said we needed to leave right away. I was all dressed up, so I hugged the kids goodbye and told them where we would be.

We arrived at El Bianco Restaurant in the town next to Westville and met five other couples, including the company president and his wife. I knew how important this meeting was for Jim, so even if I was tired, I had to rise to the occasion.

I sat next to the president's wife. This woman acted as if she thought she was really important. She was in her fifties with beautiful blue-green eyes, wearing a stylish black dress and a beautiful wrap around her thin shoulders. She talked down to all the women at the table, as if she were in charge.

All evening I listened to the women talk about themselves and their careers. The woman next to me was vice-president of her own company and had never had children. She asked me what I did, and I told her I was mother to two children and worked in a bank.

"What do you do in the bank?"

I knew I couldn't say too much, so I told her, "I'm an assistant in a small branch."

"Oh." She gave me a disdainful look. "There's no excitement in banking. I've been there."

Well! I thought. *I wouldn't say there was no excitement in banking!* But I continued to smile at her, nod, and talk about her career. Once again she referred to my job as "just working in a bank," and by the end of the evening I wanted to scream, *I'm involved in a huge under-cover FBI investigation.* But I couldn't say a word.

After dinner she introduced me to another woman who had sat at the opposite side of the table. She also wore black with a pretty shawl wrapped around her shoulders and thick gold jewelry on her arms; a huge diamond ring sparkled on her left hand. When she talked, she moved her arms, making her gold bracelets chatter. She had a superior air about her, too.

"What do you do?" she inquired.

I drew in a calming breath. "I'm an assistant at a bank." And then I just stood there while she and another woman talked about how important *her* career was. I wanted to roll my eyes, but I pretended to hang on every word.

The men were talking business, and suddenly I overheard Jim talking about the job in Europe. My ears perked up. A trip to Europe? All the women said they would be going along.

"Will you?" one asked me. I looked at them with real interest. "I wouldn't miss out on a trip to Europe." I could sure use a vacation about now, but I needed to tell Scott and Sara and find someone to stay with the kids. I could hardly wait.

The following day I drove back to the main branch and immediately went to the loan department. Every morning I saw Gerri and Deanna, who always greeted me with, "How is Mary Poppins today?" I cringed every time I heard her voice. Both of them were still up to their old antics, staying out late at bars, and apparently last night was no different.

"Mary Poppins, you should have been with us last night," Deanna gushed. "We had a blast." They continued talking about the guys they'd met, and I just walked away. I didn't want to know what they did with those 'guys.'

Today Val was showing me how loans were processed. "Make sure that when the paperwork is completed, the documents are all signed in the correct places. Otherwise, the loan will be rejected." I listened intently.

Fredric came down to the loan department on numerous occasions that day, and I noticed how close he stood to Val as they handed paperwork back and forth and how, when they thought I wasn't looking, they gazed into each other's eyes. When their conversation ended he lingered just a little too long. It was obvious to anyone they were involved.

Val said she had to run some papers upstairs to the processing department and would be back in a few minutes. I studied the loans we were reviewing, and suddenly it dawned on me that the paperwork Val should be taking up to the processing department was still in my hands.

So I went upstairs and pushed through the closed doors.

There stood Fredric and Val, locked in each other's arms, kissing like two teenagers.

I immediately averted my face. "Sorry, I didn't know you were in here."

Fredric dropped his head and Val turned beet red. I was embarrassed, but just handed Val the paperwork. "I think you meant to bring these papers up to the processing department." Then I turned on my heel and retreated down the stairs. I realized Val wasn't bringing any paperwork to anyone.

I needed to tell Scott and Sara. How many women was Fredric involved with? Were all of them doing him favors?"

Back in the loan department, I went through more papers that needed signature checks and amounts noted. Val came downstairs, still flushed. I said nothing, and neither did she. But we both knew what I had seen.

"Val, I'm going to take a short break." On my way to the teller's station, I ran into Carol, who asked me to walk out to the front.

"Rose, how is the loan department?"

Did she want me to tell her what I'd seen? Or was she just asking how my day was going? I gave her a safe answer. "I'm learning a lot."

She looked at me, then said that I was needed back at the Westville branch. "Close out over there. We're going to have Joel come over here for a meeting."

"Now? I've been in the loan department with Val all day; should I say something to her?"

"I'll take care of that, you just go."

"Carol, what if the Westville branch doesn't balance?"

She sighed. "Just keep notes on it all."

"But I don't want to be held responsible for any shortages."

"Don't worry," she said quietly. "You won't be."

When I retrieved my purse from the loan department, Val was nowhere in sight. How in heaven's name was Fredric romancing three women at work? No wonder his four ex-wives had left him!

I arrived at the branch and there was Joel, outside the bank, which left it completely unattended! This was wrong on so many levels. At least there was a camera filming so the FBI could see that he was physically leaving. I walked up the steps and Joel came up behind me.

"You're here," he said. "I'm waiting for my brother; he's in the bathroom. Then I'll go over to the meeting at the main branch."

This was a serious security breach. I buzzed myself through to the teller line and saw that Joel's teller drawer was wide open. I spun around to say something, but at that moment Joel's brother emerged from the bathroom.

"Joel," I said, you need to balance your teller drawer before you leave."

He just looked at me. "Since you only have an hour or so left in the day, just work out of my drawer."

"No, I won't do that, Joel." That was against bank procedure, and I was adamant.

He looked at me and heaved a sigh. "I'll balance it when I get back."

"Joel," I said. "Carol told me you would be over at the main branch for a few hours. I can't wait that long to balance this branch."

He slammed the teller door behind him and strode off to balance his drawer. He was obviously not happy about it, and I tried not to look at him. I was so nervous about confronting him; what if he pulled out his gun? I retrieved my teller drawer from the vault and started to count the money, watching Joel out of the corner of my eye. By this time, Miles was out front, smoking a cigarette. Thank goodness my drawer balanced.

Then Joel announced he was $1,000 short. "I don't have time to find this minor error," he said.

Minor error? I offered to recount his money for him and check his transaction receipt, but just then the phone rang.

"Rose, it's Scott," the voice said. "I'm listening to what is happening. Pretend I'm a customer."

"Oh, yes, I see."

"Before you arrived, Joel's brother pocketed some money out of his teller drawer. After you lock your drawer, go get coffee so we can see whether Joel will make him put it back."

I pretended to look up an account number on the computer screen. "Your last deposit was on the thirtieth of last month," I said in a loud voice. "Is there anything else I can help you with?"

Scott hung up and I got off the phone. "Joel, can I get some coffee while you balance?"

"Sure, sure. Hurry up, though."

I locked my drawer, walked out past his brother, and didn't look back. I went around the corner to get some tea, and when I returned, Joel announced that he'd found his mistake.

"Oh, good. Where was it?"

"In my large bills. I miscounted them."

Sure you did. *I bet you made your brother give the money back.*

Joel left the branch with Miles, and the phone rang again. "Rose, it's me again. Joel argued with Miles, and he took the money out of his pocket."

"Oh, good heavens. What if the branch doesn't balance today? What do I do?"

"At five sharp, close and lock the bank doors. I'll be watching the whole time; I'll know by your reaction if the bank doesn't balance, and I'll call you back."

Just then a woman I recognized came up to my window and stated that she was way off in her account. She was a widow in her late forties but she looked older than that, even though her hair was jet black.

"How much are you off?"

"Five thousand dollars."

"Over or short?"

"Short."

My heart sank into my stomach. I looked at her check register and said I would need to keep it for a complete review.

"Okay," she said. "Just give me another register to use in the meantime."

"Do you have sufficient funds in your account to cover any outstanding checks?"

"Yes, I do."

"Right. Then leave your register with me for a few days. It would be better if you didn't write any checks until we get to the bottom of this." She agreed, asked if she could take out a few hundred dollars to get by, and cashed a check. As she was leaving I looked up at the security cameras and shook my head. It was five o'clock sharp, so I locked the doors and proceeded to balance the bank.

Today it balanced. What a relief! Tomorrow I would need to get into that checkbook to see what was wrong. I locked the bank, set the alarm, and went out to my car. Once inside, I took my log out of my purse and made some notes. *"Make sure two people are present for balancing and locking both the vault and the ATM. Otherwise, anyone could balance and take money afterwards and the next day no one would ever know unless they balance first thing in the morning, which they don't do. For security reasons, we need to change the rules for each branch. Merchants should have their own deposit slips made out with the actual amounts."*

I dated the log and initialed it and put it back in my purse. Then I drove home.

Chapter Eight

When I reached the house, the dogs were the only ones there to greet me. In Jim's office at the back of the house I found Margaret, Anthony, and Jim working on an honors math problem. Jim turned to look at me. "How was your day?"

"Oh, you know, the usual stuff." I really wanted to shout that I'd found the loan officer and the bank president in a lip-lock, and the Westville branch manager's brother stole $1,000 and put it back when I insisted the manager balance his teller drawer.

Instead I said, "Oh, it was a typical day at the bank. I'll start dinner. How does taco salad sound?"

That night on the TV news I got the shock of my life. One of the men seen on the wharf the night that young woman was murdered had been described by a witness: Tall. Thin. Dark hair. Why, that could be anyone!

But the hair went up at the back of my neck.

The next week flew by. The woman who'd brought in her check register was in fact $5,000 short. I traced it to Joel's ID number. He'd taken the money out of her account the same day she'd brought in a check for $10,000; Joel had put only $5,000 of it into her account and pocketed the rest.

I called Scott, and he looked at the paper trail. "I see the account that this went into," he said.

"Why would Joel put this money right into his own account? That doesn't make sense."

"Looks like he's getting sloppy in covering up."

"What do you want me to do now?"

"Just credit the woman back the five-thousand."

I shook my head. "Where does this put the total number?"

Scott didn't answer.

"Can you at least tell me where all this money we're using to credit this customer account is coming from?"

"Rose, I don't want you to know more than you already do. It's for your own protection."

"But Scott, how long can we keep covering all the money that's walking out of the bank? Is there a point where we can actually do something and get Joel out of here?"

"I can't discuss that right now. Just keep doing what you're doing, Rose. I know this isn't easy for you, but you're doing a great job. I have faith in you."

Did he really think so? I looked out the bank window and saw Joel walking around in front of the bank with his brother. "Scott, wait. One more thing. There really should be two people here at all times. I feel creeped out with just Joel and me here."

"We're working on that. We need Carol here at the main branch, and you at the Westville branch. Remember, we have people watching you through the cameras all day long. They're in close proximity, so you're not alone."

I hung up the phone and Joel walked in the door with his brother.

"Hi, Joel," I managed.

"Hi, Rose. Been busy?"

"The usual." I watched Miles pick up a newspaper and then sit down without saying a word. My mind started to race. I knew I wasn't going to get answers to any of my questions today.

The bank got busy, and I was doing transaction after transaction when I looked up and there was Jim! Joel and Miles were out front smoking, but I knew Joel carried a gun and I wanted my husband to leave!

"What's up?" I said.

"Rose, we need to entertain some customers at dinner tonight. Be ready at six?"

"Six? I'll try."

"I'm going to the market to pick up dinner for the kids. Meet you at home."

I watched him walk out, praying that he wouldn't speak to Joel. Then I glanced up at the security camera. Whoever was watching me knew that my

46

husband had just walked in. This was getting difficult, and now it felt downright dangerous. How much longer would I have to do this?

I arrived at home with just enough time to freshen up and see the kids for a few minutes before Jim and I left for the evening. Thank goodness this dinner didn't last long, and we got home in time to see the kids before they headed off to bed. For me, entertaining Jim's business associates after a nerve-frazzling day at work was exhausting.

More weeks passed, and one day I realized I was always tired and my nerves were on edge. I wanted to talk to Jim. Usually I would tell him how incompetent the branch manager was, but then I'd have to stop myself before I told him what was really happening. The knowledge that someone I worked with had a gun in his pocket sent shivers up my spine. I knew that was why I wasn't sleeping at night, but I was getting really run down.

I needed to discuss this with my doctor. I made an appointment for the next day during my lunch break, and Carol came over to the Westville branch to fill in for me. At Dr. Martin's office, I described my constantly churning stomach and confessed I was under a lot of stress, but I couldn't give her any specific details. She decided to give me a complete physical.

Back at work, I peeked in through the front window of the bank and there was Carol behind the teller window. Joel sat at his desk, and there was Miles, ensconced in the lobby by the coffee machine as usual.

Carol looked up and said she would balance out so I could take over the teller station. I moved to stand at her side and she grabbed my arm. I glanced at her face and she gave her head a quick shake. "I'll be balanced in no time, Rose."

"Carol," I whispered. "Wasn't it Claire who worked this branch before you fired her?"

"Yes. She was part of this, and Joel was upset about her leaving."

"In fact," I said, "I remember that right about then people started leaving the bank, one by one, and no reason was ever given."

Carol looked at me. "The bank couldn't really say why I fired Claire, or anybody else; they were trying to keep it all hush-hush. We shouldn't be talking about any of this right now, Rose. We can talk at one of the meetings with Scott and Sara."

"Okay." I knew darn well we would never discuss anything like this in front of Scott and Sara. To protect us, they wanted to keep us in the dark about the goings on. But I grew more and more frustrated about not having anyone to really talk to.

I heard the front door close and saw that Joel and his brother had stepped outside. Very quietly, Carol asked, "How often does Joel's brother come in?"

"Every day."

"Lucky you."

I rolled my eyes.

"I'm in a rush to get to the main branch, Rose. There's a catastrophe going on there, too."

I almost laughed out loud. She didn't mean to be funny, and it wasn't, not really. We just looked at each other.

The following morning I had a hard time getting everyone up and out of the house so I could meet with Scott and Sara. Jim had an early morning meeting with clients from out of town, so I hustled the kids off to school and broke speed limits I was so anxious to get to Sweet Treat Bakery. *Be calm. Be calm.*

I finally found a parking space and ran through the door. Sara and Scott were seated at the back table, deep in discussion with Carol. Scott had papers spread out in front of him and Sara was writing in her note tablet. I took the McCall's magazine full of my notes out of my black bag just in time to hear Carol say, "I found so many discrepancies I couldn't write them all down."

Scott and Sara looked at each other without smiling. I opened my mouth and blurted, "Have any of you noticed that Fredric is fooling around with both Kallie *and* Val?"

"What?" Scott's eyebrows shot up.

"Do you think that's significant?" I asked.

"Fredric is also fooling around with Deanna," he said. "It's only a matter of time before they all find out about each other, and when that happens it won't be pretty."

I stifled a giggle. This whole thing was like a bad movie.

"Okay," Scott continued. "Let's get down to business."

One by one we voiced our concerns about our personal safety and how to cope with all the money shortages.

"We've tracked transactions to the first day Joel started work at the bank," Scott allowed. "He makes sure the amounts he takes are small enough to go unnoticed. He preys on older people who might not have good record-keeping habits, and he records only part of the money used to open a new account and pockets the difference. Now he seems to be getting careless."

"I'll say," I muttered under my breath.

"Also," Scott continued, "his brother is constantly at the Westville branch, walking money out the door."

I couldn't help asking the question that had been nagging at me for days. "Do you think Miles also carries a gun? I feel uneasy when he plants himself there all day, and I'm sure the customers think it's strange. How can we get him out of there?"

Scott frowned. "We'll have to deal with him along with all the others, all in good time. Now we have a new dilemma; people are balancing their checkbooks and finding they're short. I have twenty new cases, and we're not talking just a few dollars, either. I can't be more specific right now."

"Now what?" I ventured.

"Rose, you've stopped Joel in his tracks. He's probably trying to figure out how to get you out of there, so don't be surprised if he starts accusing you of something."

My whole body went ice-cold. "What if he gets mad and shoots me?"

The table fell silent. My God, this was turning into a nightmare!

"The local police have been notified," Sara confided. "At some point the law enforcement agencies will raid homes and confiscate any damning material. Now, remember, this is all top secret."

"And," Scott added, "just yesterday I found out these agencies might end up raiding your homes as well."

"What?" I yelped. "Seriously? Why?"

"They need to make sure no stone goes unturned," he said, his voice quiet.

"What about these magazines I use to transport copies of the accounts you have me make for you? Would that be considered taking bank property home?" I was getting more and more upset, and I could see that Carol was, too.

He heaved a long sigh. "We're working all this out with the agencies involved."

"Should we stop what we're doing?" I was thinking I might have to stop no matter what, to protect my family.

Scott was watching my face. "Don't stop," he said at last. He must have read my mind. "I'll make sure they don't raid either of your homes. I just wanted you to have the latest update."

"Rose," Carol said suddenly, "you haven't touched your breakfast."

My stomach churned. "I've lost my appetite."

Scott nodded. "You're both doing a good job. Just give us a little more time."

It sure didn't feel like I'd been doing a great job. My mind was spinning as I drove to work; I couldn't stop thinking about the what-if's. I was a wreck.

At the bank I noticed both Joel and Miles out front, smoking. I wondered if Miles knew the bank codes for the alarm system and the procedures for opening the fault. The questions made my skin crawl.

We opened the bank and got the teller drawers out of the vault while Miles sat on the opposite side of the room. A nice-looking woman walked in and I went to my window.

"Good morning. We're not quite ready to open, so could you please wait outside until nine o'clock?"

Joel interrupted me. "No worries, just wait in the lobby."

This was definitely not bank policy. I stopped what I was doing, walked out to the woman, and escorted her outside. "I'm sorry, but we'll be open in ten minutes. There's a coffee place right next door. Thanks for your understanding."

Joel was fuming when I returned. "Why did you do that?"

"It's bank policy, Joel."

"There are three of us here," he snapped. "What's the big deal?"

But Miles doesn't belong in here! I decided not to say anything and went to lock the door and finish opening up the bank.

That night when I got home my stomach was really upset, and I told Jim I needed to lie down."

"Go ahead," he said. "I'll order pizza for the kids." The thought of pizza turned my stomach.

The phone rang, and Jim brought it up to the bedroom. "It's for you." He stood there while I took the call, which made me really nervous. What if it was Scott or Sara?

But it wasn't. Instead, it was Dr. Martin, and what she said made me drop the phone.

"I'm pregnant?"

I hung up and Jim and I stared at each other. "Well, that explains a lot," I said. "I'm early in the first trimester. She says to take things easy and eat crackers for my queasy stomach and try to get as much rest as possible.

Rest! I felt like crying. "Oh my gosh, Jim, we're going to have another baby!"

"Should we tell the kids?"

"Not yet. Let's wait until after the first trimester."

He smiled. "You know you can't keep this secret."

Oh, Jim, I thought. *If you only knew what other huge secret I'm keeping!* Instead I said, "It'll be hard to keep secret for sure. Once we get past the three-month mark, then we'll tell everyone."

"This is really great news," he said softly. Then he kissed me. "I love you, Rose."

That made me feel like crying all over again.

I prayed this whole FBI thing would be wrapped up by the time I had the baby. Time would tell, I guessed. In the meantime, this was my "other" secret.

The next day when Joel was at the main branch I made a pre-natal doctor's appointment. Keeping Joel out of the Westville branch was easy for Carol; she just picked up the phone and arranged meetings. I was literally running the Westville Branch by myself, and I was proud of it.

Then one day Joel announced, "We need another teller here. My niece would be perfect." He went over to the main branch to make the request.

I never knew what happened, but Joel started blaming me for errors on accounts, and he did it in front of the customers. This infuriated me, but I had no recourse. I couldn't challenge the branch manager in front of customers. I had to tell Scott and Sara about it.

Two days later we met at the bakery and I told them Joel was making my life miserable, telling customers I was incompetent. Scott reminded me of his warning that Joel would try something like this when he felt threatened. I was upset and feeling more emotional than usual, and all at once I burst into tears.

Scott and Sara gaped at me. "What's up?" Sara asked.

"Joel's going to ruin my professional reputation," I sobbed.

Sara patted my hand. "It will work out, you'll see."

But I couldn't help wondering if it really would.

I decided to tell them about the trip to Europe Jim and I planned. They just stared at me. "You know you can't go."

I must have looked ready to cry again because Sara smiled. "We're joking," she said gently.

"How much notice will you need?" I asked.

"Make sure it's at least a week or two."

I decided to ask Jim about our Europe plans that night. I wasn't going to miss this once-in-a-lifetime trip.

When I returned to the branch, Joel and his brother were out front, talking, and a customer was inside, all alone. Wow, that's really odd, I thought. What could they be discussing that's so important?

I checked to see if the customer had opened an account or made a deposit and whether the amounts noted were correct. By that time Joel was inside, and he didn't budge from his desk for several hours so I didn't get the chance to look in his top desk drawer where he usually put new accounts.

All at once I heard his voice behind me. "Rose, I'm taking my lunch first today." I was waiting on a customer, so I nodded that I'd heard him. And then I was alone in the bank. I watched my last customer leave and decided to investigate the transaction Joel had opened this morning.

I walked over to his desk, looking for the paperwork. I found the new transaction forms but no money. But when I picked up the papers, sitting right there in the drawer was a gun.

I froze. Then I slammed the drawer shut, ran to my teller station, and got Scott on the phone. "I just found a gun in Joel's desk drawer. What should I do? Should I take it? Pretend I didn't see it?"

All at once something inside me snapped. "You need to come over here, right now!" I must have sounded frantic.

"Sara will be right over."

When I hung up I started to feel really awful. I was getting myself all worked up. *But I don't want to get shot over a simple bank transaction.* It was hard to keep from crying.

Finally I saw Sara drive up. I ran out and hugged her.

"I feel really bad," I confessed. "I'm having terrible cramps and need to use the restroom. Please cover my window."

And then I realized I was miscarrying. "Sara, I need to go to the doctor right away. It's an emergency."

She looked shocked. "Go," she said. "Go! I'll call Carol to cover here."

52

Chapter Nine

The drive over to the doctor's office seemed to take forever. *Oh, God, I'm losing the baby!* I started to cry.

Dr. Martin confirmed my worst nightmare; there was no heartbeat. I had miscarried. She told me to go home and rest. I left her office in tears, and all I could think about was how to tell Jim.

I didn't remember much about the drive home, except that at one point I turned on the windshield wipers to see through what I thought was rain. It was only a flood of tears.

When I finally got home, I called Jim at work. This was not something you ever want to tell your spouse. I was so weepy he came home early and called Carol at the bank and told her.

"Rest, Rose," he said. "You need to rest."

I blamed myself. If I had not gotten involved with the FBI and all the day-to-day stress of watching what was going on at the bank and being unable to say anything to anyone, especially Jim, maybe this wouldn't have happened. I regretted going to the police in the first place.

I guess I was in shock, just walking around in a daze.

I took the next few days off and stayed home over the weekend and just rested and thought about things. Jim and I were both devastated. One thing I knew for sure--I needed to get out of this job, one way or another. My heart wasn't in it anymore. I wanted to forget about everything happening at the bank and just stay home.

Sunday came, and I was still pretty low. Jim tried to comfort me, and the kids were so busy with school they didn't notice anything. One evening the phone rang.

"Rose, it's Sara. Can you meet on Monday morning?" Inside I groaned, but I felt I had to go.

Monday came, and I walked into the bakery to see Sara, Scott, and Carol. They all stood up and hugged me, and I tried hard not to break down. "Rose, we had no idea," Sara whispered.

"I didn't tell you because I'd just found out myself."

"Now what?" Scott asked.

I looked at him. "Now what, what?"

"Are you still going to be with us on this?"

"Do I have a choice?"

No one answered. Deep inside I knew I didn't have a choice, not really. I had to do what was right.

"We could always send you back over the main branch," Scott said. "Send Marcia over to the Westville branch."

"Can she be trusted?"

"Well," he said, "we do need two people at the Westville branch. I don't think you should be alone with Joel any longer."

"Okay. But listen, are we close to wrapping this business up?"

Again, no one answered.

"I know," I said at last, "you don't want me to know too much, right?"

Scott nodded. Their silence said it all. Then Sara handed me the magazine I used to bring them papers. "Take it easy," she said. I got up from the table and headed back to the bank.

Joel and his brother were standing out in front. *Doesn't he ever stay at home?* I wondered. "Hello, Joel. How are you this morning?"

"Good."

Miles said nothing, just stood there with his cigarette hanging out of his mouth. Joel unlocked the bank and punched in the code to open the vault. On impulse, I looked up at the security camera; it was not on.

Oh, no. Nonchalantly I surveyed the other three cameras; all of them were turned off. I didn't dare tell Joel that I knew this and I prayed Scott would realize it immediately. Customers were waiting to get inside, and at 9 sharp we let them in.

Mid-morning, Joel announced he was taking an early lunch. I nodded just as the phone rang. "Rose," Scott said. "I see the cameras are all off."

"Yes. I noticed it first thing this morning."

"Is Joel there?"

"No, he just left for lunch."

54

"Okay. Someone will be there any minute to get the cameras up and running."

At that moment a man walked in and headed straight for the cameras. Desperately I prayed that Joel would take a long lunch, as he usually did. I was busy taking care of a customer when I saw the repairman leave the branch as unobtrusively as he'd come in. I suspected it was the police again, fixing the cameras and making sure the bugs were still intact so all our conversations could be heard.

Carol walked in just as Joel returned from lunch. He was obviously surprised at seeing her. "What brings you here today, Carol?"

"Joel, we're going to send Marcia over today to be the second teller here. And," she went on," since you're getting busier with loans, we need to go over some procedures about them."

"All right." He turned away from Carol but I saw him grip the front of his jacket; his fist was clenched.

Carol spent the better part of the afternoon with me, and Marcia arrived after lunch. She was tall, wore her hair shoulder-length, and dressed conservatively. I hoped she was honest and not caught up in stealing from the bank. I showed her the small working quarters and she caught on fast.

Later, Carol took me aside. "Now you can concentrate on opening those new accounts properly. We'll deal with Joel; from now on, he'll be having a lot of meetings at the main branch. We're hoping this will result in his brother's not coming in."

I could only hope. That in itself would relieve my mind.

The days turned into weeks. Marcia quickly learned the customers' names, and they seemed to like her. What I hadn't expected was that Joel liked her, too. Very soon, Marcia was standing by Joel's desk, and they were always smiling a lot at each other. What if he got her to pilfer money to him during the day? I had to tell Scott.

Our next breakfast meeting wasn't until two days later, and until then I needed to watch carefully to see if what looked like something going on really *was* something going on. One morning I arrived at work to see Marcia and Joel standing close enough to touch and holding hands. Oh, no, not again. This was terrible.

They jerked apart when they heard me enter. "Good morning, Rose." Joel's greeting felt very awkward. After we opened the branch, both Marcia and Joel went outside for a cigarette break. That was strange; I didn't think Marcia smoked. Besides, they couldn't just run off like that; that was unacceptable bank policy.

As I left for lunch I had an inkling that something wasn't right, but I shrugged it off. When I returned, I noticed that no one at all was inside the bank! I walked in and buzzed myself into the teller station and still no one showed up. On impulse I opened the restroom door, and there were Joel and Marcia wrapped in each other's arms. Marcia's dress was half-way off.

"On, no," she yelled. "You're back!"

Joel just laughed.

I was mortified and quickly closed the door and went to my teller station, In a few moments they came out of the restroom, smoothing their clothes. "Sorry about that, Rose," Marcia said casually.

I just looked at her. *You have no idea what a creep this guy is!* I had to talk to Scott, but I couldn't use the telephone with Marcia there. Oh Lord, I wanted to be anywhere but here at the bank, and I was stuck there until five o'clock.

Things got worse. That day, Marcia did not balance; she was $2,000 short. I looked at her receipts, checked her money twice, and couldn't find an error. Joel was out front smoking, and Marcia was looking flustered. "We'll have to call the main branch for this kind of loss," I said.

"No, no," Marcia begged. "Don't do that."

Joel came in. "Rose, isn't it time for your break?"

"No," I said. "Not when I'm going home in ten minutes." But, I thought, if I leave for a minute, I'll bet the missing money will reappear. I went out to get some tea, and lo and behold, when I returned the money had reappeared. I glanced up at the security cameras; yes, they were all on. Whatever had happened had been captured on film.

I couldn't wait to get home.

"How was your day?" Jim asked when I walked in the front door. "Oh, the usual. How was yours?" I itched to tell Jim that I'd caught the new teller messing around with the bank manager. Instead I said, "You know that new teller we took from the main branch?"

Jim nodded.

"Well, she has a thing for the manager of the bank." I couldn't believe I was saying this out loud, but I reasoned that if I didn't say anything about the missing money that had reappeared, it would be okay.

"They should know better," Jim said. I agreed.

"Rose, do you have our passports?"

"They're in the safety deposit box."

"Good. Get them out. We're going to Paris in three weeks."

"Paris! In three weeks?" We were going to Europe! I smiled the whole night. Even the kids noticed the change in my mood. Nothing was going to stop me from seeing Paris. Nothing.

The following day I had a meeting at the main branch, after which I took Carol aside. "Our trip to Europe is in three weeks."

"I'll make sure the Westville branch is covered, but with the recent news from Scott, it looks like I'll be the one filling in."

I lowered my voice. "News?"

"It was bad enough that the president of the bank is involved with three women employees," Carol said quietly. "But now the Westville branch manager is involved with the new teller. And I thought she had so much promise."

"Me, too." It was a relief not to think about it any further; now it was out of my hands.

I went back to the little branch and busied myself opening new accounts and helping customers balance their checkbooks. By the time the bank closed, I was exhausted and went home to plan what I'd take on our trip to Europe.

During the next weeks, I found that more accounts had been tampered with, and Scott and Sara found that even the bank statements had been altered. Things were a real mess.

One day a man came in whom I recognized from the main office; I knew he was on the board of directors. "I was on my way home," he said, "and I realized I needed to cash this check."

The amount was for $2,000. I brought up his account on the computer screen and almost choked. His balance showed zero.

"Gerald, I need to get manager approval for this; it will just take a minute over the phone."

I called Scott. "I have a two-thousand dollar check," I said, pretending it was business as usual. "I need your approval to put the code on it."

Scott knew right away something was wrong. "Give me the account number."

I did. "I see it," he said. "Gerald Smith, right?"

"Yes."

"It's okay, Rose. Cash it. Put it in the interoffice papers for me and I'll process it today."

I gave Gerald his cash and told him to say hello to his wife for me.

"Will do." And he walked out none the wiser. But for me, such transactions weren't getting any easier. I was still shaking when the next customer came to my window.

"Rose," she said, her voice agitated. "Look at my bank statement. It shows I have two different ending balances."

Sure enough, it did show two final balances. There was a $4,000 discrepancy. I had never seen a bank statement like this one. "Can I make a copy of this and go over it with my supervisor?" I asked.

"Sure. But I hope you can credit me back the four-thousand dollar difference. I'm leaving town tomorrow and I just paid all my bills."

"Let me see your check register. Are all your checks in?"

"There are a few outstanding," she said. "But you can add them all up and see for yourself something's wrong."

I started to add and subtract with my calculator. Everything seemed to add up. "Okay," I said at last. "I'll take all this information and let my supervisor go over it. We won't charge you any overdraft fees or bounce any of your checks, and we'll get this resolved right away. Carol, from our main branch, will give you a call at home today."

"I guess I'll have to settle for that." But she wasn't happy. I felt terrible for her and right away I called Scott.

"You have to look at this statement. It's four thousand dollars short, but it doesn't make any sense; the statement shows two different balances. I looked over the checkbook register and it all seems correct."

Scott didn't say anything for a long minute.

"Whatever you do," I went on, "please don't bounce this customer's checks. She's going on vacation. I told her someone would call her when we found the correct balance."

"What a mess," he said. He hung up abruptly.

I was glad, glad, *glad* I was leaving in just a few days!

58

Chapter Ten

My sister came to stay with the kids while we would be gone. Jim's business partner and his wife, Elise, were traveling to Europe with us. At the airport the first thing out of Elise's mouth was a question about my job. "Are you still a bank teller?" Her condescending tone nettled me, and I thought about how to respond.

"As a matter of fact," I said politely, "I'm doing much more than that these days."

"I found banking to be terribly boring," she said.

"Oh, I wouldn't say it's boring," I said evenly. "I find the challenges I'm dealing with right now are overwhelming at times." I left it at that.

Our flight was announced and I jumped up. I wanted to enjoy this trip and being away from the crazy situation at the bank. I didn't intend to talk at all about my work while we were traveling. After the plane took off, Elise started reading a book; I was busy being excited and looking out the window. *I'm going to Paris!*

We flew nonstop over Iceland, and then all of a sudden we were over France. Through the darkness I could see a sprinkle of lights of the city of Paris below us, and there was the top of the Eiffel Tower! I was thrilled at the sight.

We toured with Jim's business associates, Steve and Michelle and another couple, Justin and Kirsten. I remembered them from a dinner we had attended a few months before. One day, on our way to Notre Dame and the Louvre, Kirsten asked, "What do you do, Rose?"

Oh, no, here we go again. "She's a teller in a bank," Elise answered for me. I shot her a look. Just the way she said it made me feel unimportant.

Kirsten was in charge of her own company, and we all got an earful about it.

During the days, the men had long business meetings and the woman went sightseeing or shopping. One night as Jim and I were milling around Paris after dinner, I confessed how wonderful it was to be away from the bank. He hugged me.

That night at dinner our guide, Christophe, asked each of the women what we did. I was getting really tired of that question, so I smiled and said, "I am the mother of two children."

From across the table Elise chimed in: "She's a teller in a bank."

Why was she so interested in what I did all of a sudden? I looked at Jim, but he just shrugged. He thought it was amusing that she showed such interest in what I did. I didn't think it was the least bit funny considering all the traumatic events and stress I was coping with.

Hey! I wanted to blurt. *I am helping the FBI expose a complicated embezzling scheme!* Instead I said, "Yes, and I also help manage the bank." Technically I was running the whole operation, but I couldn't explain anything more about it.

Jim and I were having a simply wonderful time; everything was so beautiful and thrilling to see! One morning we decided to see the Louvre on our own. We spent the better part of two days walking through miles of corridors where the walls were covered with paintings. I was in awe. Finally we got to the third floor where we made our way slowly down another long corridor. And there she was. The Mona Lisa.

I took a good long look at her and decided that her mysterious smile was because she hid a deep secret. The more I looked at her the more I was convinced she was hiding something. I smiled back at her. *You would not believe the secret I am keeping!*

* * *

For weeks after we returned from Europe our days and nights were mixed up. I was still euphoric over all the wonderful, beautiful things we had seen, but my first day back at work I was summoned to a meeting at the main branch. *Here we go again*, I thought.

Carol met me just inside the bank. "How was your trip?"

"Pretty fantastic," I said with a smile.

"Good. Let's go out front and talk for a minute before the meeting starts."

Instantly my nerves went on alert.

"Rose, you need to know that Fredric is no longer president of the bank."

"What? What happened?"

"One of the stockholders caught Fredric with his wife and caused a ruckus."

I just stared at her. "Any details?"

"I know the specifics," she said, "but I don't want to tell you. I'd like to keep you out of these bank fiascos."

Part of me wanted to hear all the sordid details, but I let it alone. Fredric not only had affairs with three bank employees; evidently he was fooling around with at least one of the stockholder's wives, too! That man was leading a secret life that was a huge web of deceit.

"One more thing," Carol said. "Marcia and Joel. Everyone is on to them, and Marcia's been let go. I'm afraid you'll be on your own at the Westville branch while we sort it all out."

I felt as if a truck had plowed into my stomach. "Things got worse after I left?"

She nodded. "It was really terrible."

"What about Joel?"

"He's still there at the Westville branch, but as often as I can manage it, he comes to the main branch for meetings. *A lot* of meetings."

"This all has to end soon," I ventured.

Carol agreed. "We're all tired. Scott and Sara will tell you."

At the bakery the next morning, Scott and Sara were waiting for me and they even had coffee and a small breakfast waiting. *"Bonjour,* Rose," Sara said. "I gather you had a fabulous vacation."

I grinned. "Yes, I did." And I'd leave the bank and go back in a minute, given half a chance.

"Too bad you had to come back to this mess," she sighed.

I listened to all the news and then Sara went through her files, searching for a single piece of paper she wanted to show me. "Here it is, Rose. This is the account that Joel has been filtering all the money into, with the true account number. We found it the day after you left."

I peered at it. "Take a good look at the name he's using," Scott said. "John Smith."

"How unoriginal," I quipped.

"Now we're tracing all the transactions that went from his real account number to this one. The amount of money is staggering." Sara handed me the paper. "The account number is on the back. You can refer to it, but make sure Joel doesn't see it."

"Do I understand that Joel is not only putting money into his real-name account, he has this other account, too?"

Scott nodded. "And that might not be all," he said with a frown. "We still don't have a true figure for the cash that has left the bank. But we do have an idea. Joel's brother is in the office daily, and we're trying to piece together all the transactions where paperwork is just gone. It's a tedious job."

"I can imagine," I said.

"Joel tried to hire his niece for the teller job, but we said no."

"That was smart."

Finally Sara pulled out a copy of McCall's magazine. "Can you continue what you've been doing?"

I sucked in a huge breath. "Do I have to?" I looked them both in the eye. "You guys know this goes against everything I believe about honesty. Every night I go home to my family all wound up inside, and I can't tell them anything, not one thing. My nerves are really on edge."

I took another deep breath. "Not only that, I'm working closely with someone who carries a gun. I live in fear that he might get upset one day and use it on me. I know I'm involved in a dangerous situation, but I also feel caught between doing the right thing and feeling like I'm living a lie with my family."

Sara reached over and patted my hand. "Rose, think of it this way. You're doing something really valuable for all those innocent people who have had their money stolen. You're being really brave, and because of your honesty you're helping us get to the bottom of this whole business."

I stood up. I had to get out of there and clear my head.

"Let's meet tomorrow, same time," Scott said. I just nodded without saying anything.

I began to wonder if we were meeting so we could vent our fears and frustrations to each other.

When I returned to the bank, Joel was out in front looking unusually upset. Miles was standing there, as usual. I squared my shoulders, walked into the branch, and checked to make sure the cameras were on. Yes, they were. I sighed with relief.

But when Joel stepped back inside and I opened the vault, I noticed something odd.

"Joel? Have you been balancing the vault?"

"Oh. I didn't do it last night."

Oh, my God. I had to balance the vault before I could open, and I had only 5 minutes to do it. I worked frantically, and Joel just walked back out front with his brother and pulled out a cigarette. I was going to scream!

Instead I called Scott. "The vault hasn't been balanced as of yesterday. Actually I don't know how long it's remained unbalanced. Did you know this?"

"No," Scott said dryly."

"What number do I start with?"

"Let me get Carol over there asap."

I hung up with shaking hands and balanced my teller drawer. The phone rang. And rang. I was busy, and I knew Joel should answer it, and eventually he did.

"Harvest Bank, Joel speaking." There was a long silence, and then I heard, "Yes . . . but . . . okay. All right, as soon as she gets here I'll come over."

Aha! I thought. A meeting to get him out of here."

Carol arrived, and a very unhappy looking Joel left for the main branch. She stared after him. "This situation is getting worse. I thought he was balancing the branch every day; I had no idea he wasn't."

I'd never heard Carol talk about any of this out loud. She sounded really angry.

"What do we do without a beginning balance?" I asked.

"Well, let's review the vault tape." We were huddled together counting money and trying to figure things out when a rush of customers descended. Carol decided to open up a teller drawer to help out, and when we caught up, we went back to the vault.

Both of us found that the whole time I'd been in Europe, Joel hadn't bothered to balance it. We stared at each other. "How could that be?" I asked.

Carol just shook her head. "Unless he took numbers out of thin air, I don't know."

We went back to re-check everything, and when we finished we found a huge sum of money was missing. "Carol," I gasped. "It's forty thousand dollars short!"

Instantly she picked up the phone. "Scott, you need to come over here right away. I think we need to close down this branch."

I walked over to lock the doors, but Carol stopped me. "No, we can't do that. Let's think this through, and when Scott comes, we'll figure out what to do. And as of now, if a customer comes in, make no large withdrawals."

Now I was really upset, but I just nodded. The tension in the air was thick. Customers were pouring in and I prayed no one needed to close out an existing account. I had no idea what I would tell them. I had to act as if nothing was wrong, but the truth was this was really serious, and my nerves were shot. Carol looked frazzled, too.

Scott and Sara arrived with a man I had never seen. He took a huge amount of cash out of a burlap bag. "Here. This should be enough to cover everything."

We all looked at each other as if to say, *Now what do we do?*

I rebalanced the vault as though everything were normal. Then Scott shocked me by saying casually, "Just pretend this didn't happen."

I wanted to ask where the burlap bag money had come from, but I didn't dare. I knew they wouldn't tell me, and the last thing I needed was to know one more thing I couldn't talk about to anyone.

The whole sordid thing was getting way out of control. I couldn't understand why someone didn't just fire Joel, or arrest him for theft and arrest his brother as an accomplice. Fredric was gone, and I assumed that had stopped the cash flow out of the main office. With his departure, the office affairs came to a halt. Well, at least in the main office. I was sure the FBI was watching all those involved.

Marcia was gone from my branch, and her affair with Joel had stopped during office hours, and so was the suspicion that she was stealing. But what if she tried to do what Joel's brother was doing, hanging around the bank and siphoning off cash? All sorts of scenarios tumbled around in my mind. The whole business had to come to an end sometime. I could only pray it would be soon.

Now I had more questions and no satisfactory answers. Not only that, I was an emotional wreck. It was a relief that Carol was with me during this ordeal, and when we locked up at the end of the day, I told her so.

"Rose, I wish we could discuss things further, but really, the less you know, the safer it is for you. I'll be here with you the rest of the week, but if I need to go over to the main branch, you'll be here on your own."

With Joel. My stomach turned over. I gritted my teeth and nodded. We balanced the vault again, then the ATM, and locked the bank up tight. I couldn't wait to get home.

Jim met me with a big hug and a kiss. "How was your day, honey?" I held him tighter. Today forty thousand dollars was missing from the vault, and I am so deep in this FBI sting it's making me sick.

But I couldn't say that.

"The kids are in the other room, hard at work on their homework," he said.

I tried to smile at him. "I'll start dinner." I joined the kids in the family room, where they did their homework. Margaret was working on her field study project; Anthony was studying for an algebra test. I took a seat at the table and just sat there, watching them. They were precious to me, and I couldn't let anything happen to them. I longed to stay at home and be a mom again and never have to go back to the bank.

Later I sat with Jim, watching television, but I couldn't stop thinking about the latest shortage at the bank. When was it all going to stop? When would we all be safe?

Then I thought about my mother. During World War II she had worked for the Office of Strategic Services, in the decoding department, along with Japanese analysts decoding cryptographic messages. Mom never talked about what she did during the war; she had been told to keep it all secret, and so she had.

Until the day she died, my mother never spoke of it. I knew she had dealt with life-and-death situations, but she never revealed anything about the details. Now I was trapped in the same situation, doing something I couldn't talk about. I had landed in the right place but at the wrong time, and now I found myself working under cover with the FBI. It seemed unreal.

I knew I was doing the right thing, but the price was high. The hardest part was keeping it secret from Jim and my family, and now more than ever before I understood what it must have been like for my mother. I went to bed, but I couldn't sleep.

The next day I went to the bakery for another meeting with Scott and Sara and I told them my latest suspicion. Money was disappearing into thin air. When I finished, both of them looked drained. The situation was getting to all of us, and I wondered how they were able to have any kind of a family life with their spouses or their families. I felt estranged from my family; I couldn't be honest with Jim and I was constantly evading the truth with my kids. Deep down, I was starting to wonder if the price was too high.

Finally Sara said, "Rose, you should know that the new president of the bank is part of this fraud. They did a background check on him, but he was hired before they uncovered anything suspicious.

"What? How could that be?" *Fredric is gone and now Mr. Allen was on the take?* I didn't even know his first name yet. I wondered how they figured he was involved, so I asked.

No one answered. Then I realized they knew something that I didn't.

"There will be no notification to the employees until we hire another bank president," Scott said finally. "We're looking into it."

I was blown away. Not one but two bank presidents, and all these employees, were all involved? This was one huge, awful puzzle. Things just didn't add up.

I gaped at them. "How does this kind of thing happen?"

Silence.

"Wouldn't it have been easier to just stop it a year ago, when it all came to light? I saw both Sara and Scott look at each other. Now I knew something else was happening in this banking scheme, but I couldn't quite put my finger on it.

Again, no answer. Well, maybe that wasn't surprising; I knew they couldn't tell me what they knew. After another long silence, I said, "So now what do you want me to do?"

Scott looked grim. "We need any new information. The raid will happen soon; we can't tell you specifically when, but your house won't be on the list."

"Thank God," I breathed. But no one had mentioned anything about a raid. I was afraid to ask.

Sara nodded at me. "Next week we'll have another meeting. In the meantime, do what you're doing and keep the bank and the ATM machine balanced."

"All right," I said slowly. "But I think we need to get Joel out of the Westville branch permanently. Only then will the bank stay balanced."

"All in good time," Scott said.

I drove to the office wondering about the raid Scott mentioned and when it would take place. What if no matter what Scott said, they *did* come to my house? I worried about that a lot. What would I tell Jim?

Joel was not at the bank. I went in, disarmed the alarm, got out my teller drawer, and opened the branch. I waited on customers and even opened a new account. Late in the morning, Joel walked in.

"Hi, Rose. I got tied up at the main branch."

I looked at my watch; it was 10:30. That must have been some meeting!

I'd always wondered what they had Joel doing for all those meetings he attended.

"I'll be heading back to the main branch for another meeting at four this afternoon," he said. "You'll need to close up today by yourself."

"Okay." At least I knew everything would balance! Then I realized he could come back after hours, open a teller drawer, and steal money from it. All I could do was hope for the best.

At that moment an irate customer marched up to my window. "Who do I talk to about my savings account?"

"I can help you. What's the problem?"

"I should have five thousand dollars in it, but my statement says it's zero."

"Let me take a look at your account register." I looked up his account and sure enough it said Closed. But knowing what I knew, I picked up the phone.

"Scott, please look up this account number."

I wasn't surprised when he said, "I see what happened. Rose, tell him it was human error. Tell him the money is in there and that a new statement will be generated. Also tell him he's earned interest on that money."

I sighed. "Thanks." I had no idea where Scott was getting replacement money from; I wondered if I would ever find out.

But the customer didn't let the matter drop. "This is ridiculous!" he shouted. "How could this happen?" I just stood there and kept telling him how sorry I was. Finally, he stomped out.

Knowing what I knew about the bank, I wouldn't want *my* money there, either.

Joel returned, having no idea what had just happened. I didn't tell him, either. He had missed a bank statement that should have been corrected before it was mailed, and I figured we were going to have more of these problems walk in the door. Maybe things were starting to unravel.

By 4 o'clock, Joel had left for the main branch. I finished the day waiting on customers and opened another new account. I felt comfortable doing my job, and I was getting good at going from one thing to another. I felt as if I was running the whole branch.

At the end of the day I balanced the entire bank. What a nice surprise!

Chapter Eleven

"How was your day?" Jim asked when I got home. Today I could honestly say it had been good. Then he told me he had to go to Washington, D.C. on business. His business partner, Elise's husband, was going, too.

"How's everything going with him and Elise?" I asked.

"He's divorcing her."

"Oh, that's sad. I wonder if he'd been having a fling at work?"

Jim was taking off his coat and tie. "It has nothing to do with work, honey." Then he casually mentioned that his partner had already moved in with a secretary at work.

"At work? Jim, he's not divorced yet. Moving in with an employee from work is just plain wrong."

"Yeah," he said. "Office affairs aren't a good thing."

I almost laughed out loud, but I caught myself. Even if I *could* tell him about all the bank secrets, Jim would think it was outrageous.

The next day I had a struggle getting out of bed; I was just plain tired. I got the kids to school and even had time to visit with my old favorite drive-through coffee shop. Linny was there.

"Rose! Where have you been lately?"

"I transferred to the Westville branch." I hesitated to tell her there was a coffee shop next door to the bank. I felt like a traitor. By the time I reached my little branch I had finished my coffee and needed a refill. I opened the bank and made coffee, then waited on my first customers, an older couple.

"We'd like to open a T-bill account. We just moved to this neighborhood, and we've brought a fifty-thousand dollar cashier's check."

At that moment Joel walked in. "Rose, I'll help these customers." I couldn't object, so I stood there and watched the entire transaction from my teller station. Joel was wrapping up the transaction when Miles walked in. Soon after that, the couple left the bank.

Joel seemed very happy all of a sudden, and some instinct told me to look up at the security cameras. *Now watch what he does.*

Joel put the whole amount of money in his top desk drawer. I reasoned that he took some of the money and put it in one of his own accounts and put the rest into the customer's new T-bill account. I still didn't know how the fake statements were generated.

The next thing I saw was Joel getting out a deposit slip; he wrote an amount, took another large piece of paper, and put them together. When he handed these papers to his brother, it suddenly dawned on me: That could be a deposit slip for a different bank!

It's all on tape, I thought. Scott would be sure to see it. But I checked the cameras again and the yellow light was off. They had all been disabled again, and the camera had missed Joel's putting the transaction money in his desk drawer.

Joel and Miles went out front to smoke and I called Scott. "The cameras have been turned off again."

"Damn it, not again!" I'd never heard Scott talk like that before, and it was clear he was mad.

"Joel must have come in after I closed up yesterday and disconnected them." My heart began to race.

"Rose, don't worry. We'll get them up and running, but remember, we can still hear everything that goes on over there. Joel hasn't caught on to that, yet. The police will be over during his lunch hour."

The phone rang again, and this time it was Carol. "Rose, I'm sending over a vault shipment with Ray. I want you to process it before Joel comes back from lunch today."

Later that morning, Ray walked in with the money shipment. He had me sign for the bag, and I put it on the back station table, away from the customers. Then I opened the vault and began to count out the money and finally plunged my left hand to the bottom of the bag to be sure it was empty.

When the money was counted I placed it in the vault, added the deposit amount to the vault receipt, and initialed it. Then I locked up the vault. I decided I wouldn't tell Joel about the deposit until the end of the day. I put the burlap bag aside for the paperwork that would go back to the main branch at closing time.

Joel's arrival back from lunch coincided with a flurry of customers. I didn't get to lunch for another hour, and when things slowed down I locked up my teller drawer and left, grabbed a quick bite to eat and headed back to work. When I walked in, I saw that no one was inside!

I thought maybe Joel was in the restroom. "Hello?" I called loudly.

No answer. I wondered how long the bank had been left open and unattended. I peeked inside the restroom.

Empty. I called Carol. "I got back from lunch and found the bank unlocked but no one here. I can't find Joel. I wanted you to know in case something ends up missing when I balance at the end of the day."

"Let's go ahead and balance the branch now and find out." I hung up the phone and started to do just that. To my surprise, the vault balanced, my teller drawer balanced, and so did the ATM. Carol instructed me not to balance the contents of Joel's money drawer until the end of the day.

I recorded all the figures on the daily end-of-the-day transaction and initialed the receipts as I went. All the paperwork for the day went into the burlap bag, which I set back in the vault for Ray to pick up. By then it was almost closing time and I had only a few more customers. When I finished with them, I called Carol again.

"What should I do with Joel's teller drawer?"

"He's still gone?"

"Yes."

"Hmmmm." There was a long pause. "Rose, I'll drive over to your branch. I'll be there in case he does show up, and I'll bring a master key to open his teller drawer."

By the time she arrived, Ray had picked up the end-of-the-day paperwork and driven it back to the main branch.

"Still no Joel?" Carol inquired.

"No."

She shook her head.

"I didn't know what to make of it," I said." By this time it was 5 o'clock, and I locked the front door.

"I guess tonight we'll have to balance his teller drawer for him," Carol said angrily. "I've never had to use the master key, so I hope this works."

We were both surprised that the drawer actually did balance. We finished all the paperwork, put everything back into the vault, set the alarm, and stepped out front. But as we said goodnight, I spotted Joel's car.

"Carol, look over there! Joel's in his car with Marcia!"

"Let me take care of this," she said. "Wait here until I come back." She started for his car.

I had no idea what she said to Joel, but he started his engine and his tires squealed as he roared off.

"I told him to report to the main branch until further notice," Carol said. "Rose, you're running this branch by yourself now. Until we decide what the next step will be, you're in charge."

In charge? Wow, I was running the whole branch myself! I could hardly wait to tell Jim.

At home, Jim was just taking off his suit jacket and the kids were already doing homework. "How was your day, honey?"

I thought about that for a minute. I could say that the bank manager had left the branch completely unattended, which was a security breach. But then I thought that saying this might lead to more questions about Joel.

"I had a really busy day, opening accounts and processing them." *And I am now in charge of the Westville branch.* I didn't tell him because I couldn't tell him why.

The next morning the kids were next to impossible to get out of the house. I hit the snooze button one too many times and I knew we'd all be late if we didn't rush. By the time we got in the car no one was in a good mood, and we drove in silence. I sped down each street like a race car driver.

I had no idea whether the kids were late, but it must have been close. By that time I was dragging and really needed my coffee, so I drove over to the Real Caffeine drive-thru and sat patiently in my car thinking about what was happening at work. Suddenly I remembered I had an early meeting with Scott and Sara at the bakery.

By the time I reached the pickup window I was in such a rush I gave Linny my money, thanked her, and drove off. Without my coffee. I thought about stopping and going back, but I was already late. Then I glanced in my rear-view mirror and saw Linny leaning out the pickup window with my coffee in her hand, waving at me. Another car had taken my place in line, so I just drove on.

I was losing my mind.

I got to the bakery and Sara asked me for the paperwork I had. As I dug the magazine out of my big purse, out tumbled the photos for Margaret's field study project; they spilled all over the floor.

Scott picked one up and stared at it. "Rose, what is this a picture of?"

I looked at it closely. "It's from my first day at the Westville branch. It's a photo of the vault documents that first day when it was $60,000 short."

"There are Joel's initials for the vault from the day before, with the date of the incident." He bent closer. "The vault was balanced with his initials the day before. Rose, this is concrete evidence! Those are his initials right there! And there's the date. It's amazing that you had the foresight to take these pictures!"

Scott then went through the rest of my photographs and saw the one of the ATM receipt. "Amazing! We've hit the jackpot."

They all huddled over the table, looking at the photo of the balancing vault receipt and ATM receipt, talking nonstop about things that made little sense to me. I had no idea what it all meant, but *they* sure seemed to.

Scott gathered up all my photos. "You can't take those photographs," I protested. "Those are for my daughter's biology field study project."

"I'm sorry, Rose. This is evidence. I need to keep them."

"Just give me back the ones of bugs and water and other things."

Scott shook his head.

"What about giving me the negatives?"

"Sorry, Rose. We need the complete package with the date they were processed and the exact number of photos involved."

That really got to me. What would I tell Margaret? I was so upset I got up to leave and left my McCall's magazine sitting on the table.

"Do you have the developing envelope, too?" Scott asked.

I looked in my purse and reluctantly gave them the envelope, which was dated. "Please let me have the bug photos. Please?"

Scott really did look sympathetic. "I'm sorry, Rose. We need to keep this all intact."

"I wish I hadn't come in today!" I blurted. "You have no idea how much work my daughter has done for that project. If I'd known you were going to confiscate them, I would have brought in only the two you're interested in."

No one said anything, so I grabbed my magazine and left. I couldn't tell Margaret the FBI had taken her field study photos; that would blow the cover off everything. I sure hoped no shenanigans would go on at the bank today; I just wasn't in the mood for it.

When I arrived, there was Joel out front, smoking with his brother. *Wait a minute! Joel's supposed to be at the main branch.* I didn't know what to do in front of his brother, so I just said, "Good morning, Joel."

"Hello, Rose."

Laura arrived just as I was opening the branch. She looked right at Joel. "Carol said for you to go straight over to the main branch."

"Oh, I'll get there in a few minutes. I have some work I have to get."

What work did he need to get? Whatever it was, it was probably in his top desk drawer.

The phone rang and Carol was on the line. "Rose, is Joel there?"

"Yes, he is."

"Put him on, please."

"Joel, it's for you."

He turned to me. "Just tell them I'm busy opening up the branch."

"Joel, I'll open the branch. I think you should take this call."

Reluctantly he picked up the phone. "Joel here." His face went beet red and he started to stammer. Then I heard him slam down the receiver. He didn't say a word, just stomped out the door with his brother.

Laura and I opened the branch and found everything balanced just the way it should be. I looked up as customers started to enter, and even the cameras were working!

One man came in to open a new checking account. I went over to Joel's desk and opened the top drawer to get a new account form, and there were a number of unprocessed new accounts, just sitting there. *So this is what Joel wanted to pick up before he left.*

I checked the dates. Some of them went back as far as a month ago. *Those weren't here the last time I looked in this drawer.* Then I looked for the money that correlated with the account numbers.

I called Scott. "I found fifteen new accounts opened in the past month just sitting in Joel's desk drawer. The problem is, the money is not matching up with the accounts. No cash is here, either."

Scott groaned.

"Not only that," I continued, "I looked on the computer and none of them have even been processed!"

"They weren't entered into the computer at all?" he said in a tight voice.

"Not that I can see."

"I'll come over and take a look. Don't say anything in front of Laura."

"She's at lunch right now."

"Good."

When Scott arrived he opened Joel's desk drawer while I waited on customers. When I looked over, he had the new accounts spread all over the desktop; it looked like he was trying to put a puzzle together.

"I have no idea which ones should have cash or checks," he said, shaking his head.

"You know what I think?"

He glanced up at me with interest.

"I think all along Joel's been giving these new accounts to his brother, and then they walk out of this bank and go to another bank, or to his home. I think if you guys got into his house, I bet you'd find a lot of evidence."

Scott looked like he wanted to tell me something, but he didn't. "I'll take these with me to the main branch and get some kind of explanation from Joel."

That was the first time I'd heard anyone was going to ask Joel point blank about the accounts that had money missing before they were entered into the bank system. Just then Laura walked in the door.

"Anything interesting happen while I was gone?"

I almost choked. "Not too much, no." *You just missed the FBI, and Joel had 15 accounts in his top drawer and the money doesn't add up.*

The rest of the afternoon flew by and I breathed a sigh of relief. It was such a good feeling not to worry about Joel's antics at the end of the day. It wasn't until I got into my car that I noticed the diamond was missing from my wedding ring. Stuck in the prongs was a little brown piece of burlap.

When could I have lost the stone? Then I remembered two days before, when I'd handled the vault money; maybe it could have lodged inside the courier's burlap bag.

I felt just awful when I got home. Jim looked at me over the newspaper he was reading. "What's wrong, honey? I guess he could tell by my face that something was not right.

"I've lost the diamond from my ring." I held up my left hand with my wedding band and my engagement ring with the empty setting.

"Let me see. What's that brown string in the setting?"

"Burlap. I think I lost it two days ago when I took money for the vault out of a burlap bag."

"You're just noticing it now?"

"I guess so." I couldn't confess how distracted I'd been the last few days about Joel and the bank.

"Tomorrow at work you can just look in the bag," he suggested.

"It's not that easy, Jim. The courier took the bag with all our paperwork from that day back to the main branch. I have no idea where that particular bag is." I started to cry. "That was my engagement ring!"

Jim hugged me. "We'll get you another diamond."

"I want my old diamond back! You hand-picked that diamond for me."

That night Margaret didn't ask me about the photos for her field study project, and I wasn't about to volunteer any information until I had to. I still didn't know what I was going to say.

The following day I went straight to the main branch to check in all the burlap bags. I found four and turned them all inside out. No diamond. I asked everyone who had access to them if they'd seen my diamond, and in no time I had everyone at the bank looking for it. When Carol heard what had happened, she shook her head.

"Oh, Rose, that's really too bad. I'll make sure all the tellers are alerted and I'll talk with Ray and look in our vault. I'll also go up to the proof department to see if maybe it was left in one of the burlap bags or on the floor, or even on the carpet."

"But housekeeping comes in at night; my diamond could have been sucked up by a vacuum cleaner."

I was heartsick when I left for the Westville branch. Laura was standing outside. She was a really nice woman, very friendly with the customers. We got along well; I would open the accounts and she would process them. The day went smoothly. *Now this is what banking should be. A fine-tuned operation.*

At the end of the day the phone rang. "Well, Mary Poppins, is Laura there?"

I cringed. It was Deanna from the main branch. "It's for you, Laura."

She listened, then asked me if I wanted to meet the girls from the main branch for drinks at The Drinking Hole.

"Not tonight, Laura." I didn't feel like talking, much less laughing over drinks.

When I got home that night, Jim met me when I pulled into the garage. "Honey, it looks like we have a problem with the roof in Margaret's room."

"What?" This was the last thing I needed. I went into the house where the kids were, and Margaret looked up from her homework. "Mom, did you get my field study photos? I need to start labeling them."

She'd caught me off guard. Oh, Lord, what was I going to say to her?

I hedged. "Let me see if they're in the car." This was just awful. I went back into the house and sat down beside her. "Margaret, I'll hop in the car and see if I can pick them up for you."

"Thanks, Mom."

I left the house feeling dreadful and dishonest and drove around and around wondering what I could say when I returned. I was gone for 30 minutes.

"Margaret, they don't have your photos." Well, that was true enough. I just couldn't tell her who *did* have her photos.

"What?"

"I think you'll have to retake them."

Margaret looked really upset until Jim chimed in. "Margaret, I can help you go back to the place we looked at. It will be easy to re-shoot some of those pictures."

I just listened. I felt terrible, really terrible. But I couldn't very well say, *"Oh, by the way, your photos have been confiscated by the FBI."*

Chapter Twelve

The next morning we had a meeting at the bakery to discuss Joel. "There's a new development," Scott began. My stomach tightened. *Oh, now what?*

"I want to bring Joel back to the Westville branch," Scott began. "He's starting up questionable things with his brother at the main branch. We haven't been able to capture any trade-offs yet, but we can have better control at the little branch."

"Can we really trust Joel any place?" I asked.

Everyone looked at me.

"I don't think I can stand the threat of Joel's gun anymore," I added. "Do you know if he's still carrying it?"

Scott sighed, and I went on. "Last night I had to lie to my daughter about her field study photos. Now she has all the extra work involved in taking new ones, and it makes me feel terrible. I feel like a bad mother. And on top of that, I have to worry about a thief with a gun at my work place? I want to go home every night to my family. Don't you guys understand that? My life is anything but normal, and I can't talk about it to anyone!"

There, I'd said it out loud.

No one spoke. They all just sat there and stared at me. Finally Scott took a sip of his cold coffee. "We're working on it, Rose. Really we are."

"Listen," I said. "I need a week off work to get the roof repaired on my house."

"When?" Carol asked.

"In three weeks."

"Sure, you could take some time off. In the meantime, Joel is going back to the Westville branch."

The next few weeks went by fast. Joel was back up to his no-good ways and I was not only scared, I was frustrated. One day I looked up and the cameras had been dismantled again.

I got on the phone. "Scott, the cameras aren't working. Again."

"I noticed. Someone is on his way." And just then a man walked in and headed straight for the cameras.

"Joel still hasn't figured out that we have the office bugged," Scott said.

"Thank God for small favors." But it was only a matter of time.

"You have one more week before you go on vacation, right?"

"Right. Who are you sending to cover for me?"

"We'll discuss that at our meeting tomorrow."

Since Joel was back in the office, I tried to make sure I opened accounts at my teller window to prevent him from stealing any more money. His brother showed up every day, always with a newspaper in his hand. At some point Joel would watch me to see when I looked away and then he'd take things out of his desk drawer and give them to his brother. I couldn't believe he thought I wasn't noticing his actions.

The week before I left for vacation, one of my regular customers came to my window. "Rose, my bank statement is way off."

"What's the problem? I knew exactly what the problem was; her account was short.

"My account is two thousand dollars short."

"Let me see." I took her statement and check register and went to work. "This may take me awhile to find out where the error is. Can I copy this statement and keep your register?"

"You know, Rose, this is the second time this year this has happened. I wasn't really short the last time, and I know I'm not this time."

"I understand, and I'm sorry for your inconvenience. I'll make sure that all the interest earned will be updated."

The next morning we all met at the bakery and I brought a copy of the customer's statement. "Look at this," I said. "It looks correct, right? Now look where the teller stamps it." I flipped the register to the front. "It's the same. Now look at the statement; it shows a different deposit amount! And look at the coding next to the deposit on the statement—it doesn't match any of the bank's codes. It's a wonder people haven't been bouncing checks all over town!"

"People *have* been bouncing checks all over town," Carol said dryly.

"They just don't know it. We're intercepting most of them, but this particular statement got past us."

"Would you all agree that Joel must have access to a computer someplace to do this outside of bank hours?" I asked. "He's always out front smoking and rarely uses the computer at work. Do you think he sneaks back after hours?"

"Possibly," Carol allowed. "It's a real mess."

"He's not using a bank computer," Scott said. "We've found the computer on-line; we just haven't found it physically yet."

"That's why we have computer specialists all over the bank working overtime," Sara added.

I couldn't believe what I was hearing.

"When Joel was at the main branch we discovered he was taking teller work, walking out the door, and bringing it to the Westville branch. And vice versa."

I just shook my head. *Why don't they just fire the guy? There must be more to this.* "I need to know how to credit this customer back and from what account."

"Give it to me," Carol said. "I'll do it first thing when I get back to the office and send it with Ray when he picks up the teller paperwork."

"I *knew* I was on to something." I practically crowed with delight.

"I can't believe you found out all that information by yourself, Rose."

I passed my McCall's to Sara. "Here are the accounts and copies of what you asked me to get."

Scott gazed at me, an odd expression in his eyes. "You really are making a difference in the amount that's being taken. We want you to know you're doing a good job."

I longed to ask if Joel would be gone when I came back from vacation, but I didn't dare. This problem was more complex than I could ever have dreamed.

Friday came, and was I glad I was taking a week off from all this commotion! I called the contractor during my lunch break and he was all set to go to work. I balanced the vault, the ATM, and my teller drawer and Joel did the same. He had put some new accounts in his desk drawer, and I knew I should call Scott to tell him, but it was 5 o'clock and I was officially on vacation. I took one more look at the cameras to make sure they were on, and then Joel and I set the alarm and left.

"Have a good vacation," he said.

"Thanks, I will." Wait until he arrives Monday morning and finds out Carol will be here while I'm gone. His reaction wouldn't be fun to watch.

By the end of the week, the contractors had put on the new roof, painted the garage, and repainted the ceilings in the family room, living room, hallway, and Margaret's room. Overseeing the workers was such a welcome relief from being at the bank with Joel.

The day I returned to the bank I found Carol standing outside. "Rose, how was your vacation?"

"It was a working vacation for sure, but the new roof is on. And it was less stressful than being here at the bank." Then I asked, "Where is Joel?"

She winced. "He's at the main branch all week."

Something had happened while I was on vacation, I could sense it. But I wasn't sure if I should ask. But I did. "Carol, what happened while I was gone?"

"The bank is being audited," she said shortly.

"Oh? And?"

"Rose, the less you know, the better for you. Meet us tomorrow at the bakery. Things are getting worse, and Scott will be calling you."

My chest tightened. I was right back in the middle of the muddle. "Do I still do what I've been doing?"

"Yes," she said with a sigh. "Until we hear otherwise from Scott."

We were busy until lunch, and she suggested I eat in the office in case the auditors showed up. "We need two people here at all times."

They didn't show. At the end of the day, everything balanced and we both left. That night I asked Jim the question that had nagged at me all day.

"Why is it a bad thing to be audited?"

"Auditors want to find out if there's anything wrong," he said. "Why?"

"The bank is being audited."

"Banks and publicly held corporations are required to have audits; that's to protect the stockholders. Did someone call them in?"

I just stared at him and sat down hard on the sofa. *Oh my God, this whole thing is going to blow up.* The auditors will find all the discrepancies I've been finding. Would they shut down the branch? Would anyone be arrested? What if it's not the people at fault?

I tried to calm myself down, but my thoughts were in chaos. Would I be implicated? I didn't think my nerves could take any more of this; maybe I should call Scott right now.

Jim was saying something, but I wasn't concentrating. He looked at me.

"What do you think of that?"

"What?"

"Weren't you listening?"

"Sorry, Jim, I had a really long day and I'm really tired."

"I was saying I have to go to Texas next week on business."

"Okay." In a daze I went into the kitchen to start dinner, still fretting over the audit. *What if they think I'm the bad guy?*

When we sat down to eat, Margaret announced she was almost finished with her field study project. "It's a good thing I had time to re-take all those photos."

I almost dropped my fork. "Yes, you're lucky you had time."

That night I lay in bed with my mind spinning. Things couldn't get any worse, could they?

Little did I know.

In the morning I drove to the bakery in a rush because I couldn't wait to hear what was going to happen with the audit. Scott met me in the parking lot. "You're here early, Rose."

"Carol told me about the auditors."

He sighed and rubbed his chin. "Yes. Let's go on in and order some coffee."

Both Carol and Sara looked exhausted when they arrived. As soon as everyone had their coffee, Scott cleared his throat. "You all need to stop what we've been working on and be extremely careful not to take any documents out of the bank. The auditors will see the computer trail."

I gulped down a swallow of my coffee. "What are you going to do about Joel?"

"I have a feeling this house of cards is coming down around him."

That made me sit up straight and look directly at him. Scott *never* talked like this in front of us.

"Now that the auditors are in the bank," he said quietly, "it's just a matter of time before they find something."

"Will we be implicated?"

Scott just sat there. Carol carefully set down her coffee mug on the table. "How do we protect ourselves if we *are* implicated? Do we just come right out and tell them what we already know?"

My thoughts exactly.

"We will step in," Scott said, resignation in his voice. "But I cannot give you any details. But that doesn't mean a lot of questions won't be directed to you. It may get very uncomfortable."

I began to squirm. "Do we tell them you guys are from the FBI?"

"No." He sat without moving for a long minute. "I will be stepping in at some point, but again I can't be more specific. If the auditors see what we've been seeing, they will see who is responsible when they research the codes and manager ID number. Just do your job as though nothing is going on."

"But . . . "

"We'll talk when the auditors are gone, but don't ask me when that will be. And don't ask anything else about Joel. I can't discuss it."

Carol and I looked at each other. The tension in the room said it all. We had this meeting to urge us not to talk about what the auditors might or might not uncover, and we should be prepared to answer questions without implicating the FBI? How in the world was this going to turn out?

I went over to the Westville branch and ran into Joel, who had just driven up. "Good morning, Joel," I said as we made our way to the front door.

"Hi, Rose." We went in and set up for the day as if everything was perfectly normal. The day went well until a slim man in a dark suit came in and showed Joel his identification card.

"I need complete access to this branch," he announced. It had to be one of the auditors!

Chapter Thirteen

Joel sat at his desk, and I buzzed the man into the teller station where the vault was. "Hello," he said to me. "My name is Paul, and I will be balancing the branch now."

"My name is Rose," was all I could think of to say.

"Is there a code you can put into the vault so I can balance it?"

"Yes. Let me do that for you; an alarm will go off and then you can get into the vault."

When the alarm went off I asked if I could take out my teller drawer and continue to wait on customers.

"Yes," he said. "Work as though I am not here." I took my teller drawer out and double-checked to be sure all my cash was there. I noticed that Paul was busy counting and writing things down, and that made me nervous.

I went ahead and waited on customers, but all the while I kept a close eye on the auditor. He sure wrote a lot of things down. Finally he walked over to the ATM machine and I prayed to God it was still in balance. I tried not to look nervous, but I was shaking.

I looked over at Joel, and he was fidgeting in his desk chair and scratching his arms. It was obvious he was a wreck. Joel was a piece of work. He spent the better part of the day smoking outside, and I had absolutely no respect for him. And his brother, Miles, was even worse. I wondered if Miles would show up today while we were being audited. And I sure wondered if Joel could manage Miles if he did turn up. I was disgusted at the whole sordid business.

And the tellers were having affairs with bank executives? What did they think they were doing? It made me mad because it affected me—boy, did it affect me!

My emotions were all over the place. When I thought about all this, I realized it was sheer luck that I happened to go to the police, which brought in the FBI. If another teller had been sent over to the Westville branch that day, who knew how much more money would have been stolen out of customer accounts?

Then I began to worry about who would be harmed? Would the bank have to close? I went into the restroom just to calm down and found myself staring in the mirror. *What the heck have I got myself into?*

Customers were coming in, and I had to get busy. Then Paul asked for any outstanding loans or T-bills or savings or checking accounts. At that very moment, Joel was involved in opening a new account; I looked up from my station and hoped to God his desk drawer was not full of month-old accounts.

Joel took the account he had just opened and handed it to Paul. "This is the only outstanding account." Paul inspected it, inspected the entire branch, inspected my teller drawer, and asked to see the other teller drawer still in the vault. I went to get it.

"Joel, you need to open your teller drawer for Paul." And I began to sweat. *Please let it balance today. Please!* Joel opened his teller drawer and, wonder of wonders, it did balance!

Three hours passed and finally Paul said, "I need to take all this information to the main branch. Thank you for your cooperation." And he was gone.

"Wow," Joel exclaimed. "He was a man of few words, wasn't he?"

I just nodded. My mind was racing. *What had Paul found?*

The auditors worked at the main branch for over two weeks, and rumors were flying. No one was talking about what they were actually finding, but I suspected both the managers and the stockholders were getting an earful.

Lately I'd noticed that Joel's brother was staying away from the Westville branch and Joel seemed to be doing his bank work. Maybe he'd noticed the security cameras and decided he needed to behave. The next several weeks seemed perfectly normal, but I couldn't help wondering what would come next.

One night at home I received a call from Scott to set up a meeting. The following morning I drove to the bakery and turned into the parking lot just as Scott entered. He stayed in his car collecting papers; I went in and ordered coffee. Carol and Sara finally appeared, and we waited for Scott.

When he joined us the first thing he said was, "I can't discuss the auditors' findings, but I can tell you that they had a long meeting with me." He was talking slowly and methodically, and Carol and I perked up and listened intently.

"Where do we go from here?" Carol inquired.

Scott looked at me. "Rose, I want you to run the Westville branch, as you have been doing. Keep track of accounts with any discrepancies we might have overlooked. Carol, keep an eye on the tellers' work at the main branch, especially the balancing procedures. Everything must be done by bank rules. I can't go into what the auditors actually found, but you can pretty much guess."

Everyone was unusually quiet. "What is going to happen with Joel?" I asked.

Scott took a deep breath. "Last night there was a raid."

My jaw dropped open.

"The law enforcement agencies went into Joel's house. They found evidence and Joel was taken into custody."

Stunned, Carol and I just sat there, and suddenly tears of relief began to well up. "Oh, thank God, this is the end of it!"

But Scott leaned toward me with a serious look. "This is not the end. The hard part is just starting. We found extensive and damning information, paperwork that should never have left the bank in the first place, along with a lot of money and the computer Joel used to alter statements. Needless to say, he will no longer be working at Harvest Bank."

Carol and I gasped and started talking at once. "Wait a minute," Scott interrupted. "This doesn't mean it's all over. Let me tell you what this does mean."

"Why not?" I must have looked puzzled because Scott looked straight at me.

"We have to prosecute him. Rose, we might need you to testify against him."

It didn't hit me right away, but when it registered, I burst into tears. I was going to have to let Joel know I was the one who had exposed him? My family would be put in harm's way because of me, because I'd gone to the police in the first place. I thought I was going to faint.

Sara moved over to my side of the booth and Scott took my hand. I was shaking.

"This means Joel will find out what I knew all along?" I asked.

"Yes."

"No. I can't risk that. I'm afraid Joel's brother might come after me."

Scott leaned over and said, "Joel's brother was also taken into custody."

"But what if one of them gets out of jail? They both know I was there and watched everything they did."

"Rose, they don't know it was you for sure."

"Does anyone else know about me?"

"No. Only Carol."

"What about Fredric? Remember, I went to him with my suspicion in the beginning."

"He's already pled guilty, Rose."

"What? When did that happen? What if he told someone else about me?"

Scott could see me putting two and two together. "Don't think the worst. Joel thinks it's Fredric who set him up. What Fredric didn't count on was that by bringing in Joel, he also brought in Miles, who was involved with drugs." He stopped, frowned, and then went on. "I know I shouldn't have told you that, but you need to know so you can testify against Joel. We're going to put him and a few others away for a very long time."

"Enough!" I said. I was furious at them for putting me in this situation. They didn't know who I was, who my family was. They didn't know what was at stake for me. I had never been so mad.

"You have some nerve using me as a pawn like this was some kind of game!" I was almost shouting.

"It's no game, Rose," Scott said. "I know this whole thing is unfair to you, but I swear I'll put so much pressure on Joel and Miles and Fredric that they'll turn against each other. I hope this will be before you'll have to testify. But remember this, if you *don't* testify, Joel may walk away a free man."

Questions flooded my brain. Could I confront those people in a courtroom? What would happen to my family? "Scott, what if they don't get prosecuted? What if they are found not guilty?"

"No chance of that. There's a drug ring involved; that's where Miles came in. It's an open-and-shut case. And you have my word that we will protect you."

Oh, God. If Jim found out he would move our family away from here.

"I need to think this over. You need to tell me exactly what this means for me and my family. Before I say yes or no, I need these answers."

Carol tried to change the subject, but my mind couldn't focus on anything else. Wasn't it enough that I'd lived through this whole thing? Now I had to testify in court?

Scott grew quiet. "I can't go into detail now, but it's likely that a new president will come in. This is much larger than grand theft larceny."

My stomach sank down to my toes. "I don't think I can go through with this. I want some assurance that my family stays safe from harm."

Carol looked at me and Sara laid her hand on mine. Scott nodded. "I'm sorry it has to be this way, Rose. I really am."

I believed him, but so what? I almost walked out then and there. "Now what?" I was still shaking so hard I was afraid to pick up my coffee cup.

Scott looked at each of us. "This will take some time to sort out. In the meantime, I need you to continue to do your job."

I left the bakery and drove straight home to settle my nerves. When I walked in the house I saw all the photos of Jim and the kids and our parents and I started to sob. *You have to get a grip on yourself, Rose.*

I didn't want to go back. I didn't want to set foot in the bank ever again. The phone started ringing, and I just let it ring and ring and ring . . . finally I picked it up, and it was Scott. He and Sara were at the Westville branch, waiting for me to return. They had guessed I was ready to escape.

I repaired my makeup, got in my car, and drove slowly to work. On the way I thought about what was happening and what I was going to tell Jim if I had to testify in court.

I had known something was going to happen; I just hadn't known that I would be involved.

My nerves were shot. Worst of all, I still couldn't tell Jim anything because Scott said not everyone involved had been arrested yet. I felt sick with anxiety.

I opened the branch and Laura came over from the main branch to help. "Good morning, Rose. How are you?"

I wanted to scream. *I just found out that convicting Joel depends on my testimony.*

That day went by in a blur. I got home that night, and there was Jim. I dropped my purse on the floor and hugged him. "Hi, Rose. How was your day?"

He always asked that, and I couldn't begin to tell him. I started to cry.

"What's wrong?" he said sharply.

Now was not the time to explain anything; I had to pull myself together.

"I had a really, really bad day. Nothing seemed to go right." At least *that* was the truth.

"You're home now, honey. You can forget it for a while."

I hugged him again. Oh, if only I *could* forget it!

The phone rang. I picked it up and heard Scott's voice. "Sara and I could see how upset you were today. I just want you to know we're doing everything we can to keep you from having to testify. You have done an outstanding job, Rose; we want to do what we can for you."

I said nothing, just hung up the phone. "Who was that?" Jim asked.

"Someone from work who had just as bad a day as I did." *And that was true, too.*

I didn't sleep much that night, wondering what the next day would bring. All I could think about was testifying against Joel.

There was a staff meeting at the main office that morning. Carol nodded at me, and I could see she was upset, too. Scott and Sara were there, and when we were told about the findings of the audit, our eyes met across the room. Then the new bank president introduced himself and said that in the next few weeks he hoped to meet each of us. All I could think about was the last president, Fredric, who was involved in this whole mess.

When the meeting adjourned, Laura and I drove to the Westville branch. I entered the parking lot and oh my God, there was a man who looked exactly like Joel! Could he have been released already?

I called Scott right away. "I think I saw Joel in the parking lot," I whispered into the phone.

"Not possible. Joel is locked up tight for right now."

"What do you mean 'for right now'? Could he get out before his court date?"

"Not if I can help it."

I had a terrible feeling someone was watching me, and I kept looking around to see who it was. Just the thought gave me chills.

A customer came into the branch and wanted to open a time certificate. I locked up my teller drawer, walked over to the desk, got out my pen, and looked in the side drawer of Joel's desk to get the application forms. When I started to open the account I found I needed a verification stamp, so I opened another drawer. Sitting right there in the back were a few new account forms that had account numbers but no money attached. I was sure we had gone through all the drawers; had someone come into the bank and put them there?

The instant Laura left for lunch, I called Scott again. "There are two new accounts that I don't remember seeing the last time we looked through the desk."

"That's odd. Let me look at your branch camera records and get back to you." At 4 o'clock that afternoon Scott walked in with two other men, and a minute later Carol called and asked Laura to come to the main branch for a meeting. Laura left immediately.

When the office was finally clear of customers, Scott said to the men, "Start working."

Something had happened. The front door was taken off its hinges and a new one installed. One of the men came around to the vault and started to do something inside. I looked over at Scott.

"As of today we needed to put in new security measures," he explained. "New codes. New door." He didn't elaborate. By the time the new access code was ready to use, I balanced the vault and ATM and my teller drawer. Scott and the two men stayed until closing time. As I was leaving, Scott took me aside.

"Joel had us bugged, too," he confided. "But we knew about it. Today we saw his sister come into the bank before opening hours; she must have gotten all the codes from Joel. We picked her up. We didn't want to take any more chances of someone else illegally entering the bank."

I couldn't say a word. Scott tried to smile. "I know this is hard on you, but I want you to know you are being watched. No one is suspicious of you. Try to have a good night."

Try to have a good night? Was he kidding? I was blown away at the thought of what could have happened. I went home and tried to forget the whole mess. My stomach was feeling very unsettled, and I decided I needed to get something for my nerves. How could I begin to tell my doctor about what was going on?

From then on, I began having the recurring nightmare I'd had ever since Margaret was born. I'd wake up in a cold sweat, and I'd remember every single detail of something that had happened years ago. On a cold February day around noon, Jim and I are on our way home from Memorial Hospital with our beautiful new baby girl, wrapped up in a hand-knit pale yellow sleeper and a matching baby cap. She is lying peacefully asleep in the brand new car seat Jim had installed in the back of our blue Monte Carlo. I am tired after delivering the baby, and Jim is excited about bringing us home.

The sky is overcast and snow is starting to fall. All the trees are bare, and the roadside has two feet of built-up snow, which is black from the dirt kicked up by cars driving by. I'm anxious to get home with Margaret, and I keep looking into the back seat to make sure she's all right; Jim is talking about how wonderful it is that she's finally here and what a beautiful baby she is.

But suddenly, out of the corner of my eye, I see a red four-door sedan drive up beside our car, speed past, and make a U-turn. Now it's coming back toward us, and I can see that the driver has only one hand on the steering wheel and he's laughing. Just when he comes abreast of us, I see he is waving something out the window.

He has a gun! "Watch out," I yell to Jim. The man points the gun right at Jim, then at me, and mouths the words, "Bang, bang." He drives away and Jim pulls over and stops.

"That man had a gun!" I shout to Jim.

"I know," he says. He is shaking, and we both look back at Margaret and then at each other. And that's when I wake up.

Often this dream woke me out of a sound sleep and then I lay awake thinking about what could have happened that day. Lately I'd been having this nightmare a lot more often.

I made another appointment with my doctor and told her the kind of stress I'd been under and that things were turning upside down at work. She wanted me to get some counseling, but I didn't have the time between my job and the early-morning meetings at the bakery.

She examined me and said to come back the following week. And if I didn't feel better before then, she would give me something for anxiety.

At the next meeting at the bakery Scott looked relaxed. *What was going on now?* I wondered. Being at the Westville branch kept me away from all the activity at the main branch.

"Things are coming to a head with Joel's case," he said. Then he asked, "What are you planning to do about testifying against Joel and his brother?"

I just looked at him. "I don't know. I really don't know."

"We need to know this week."

I told him I would have an answer for him soon. Actually I had given it so much thought I was making myself sick.

At the bank that day, Carol confided something astounding. One of the main branch tellers had a customer come in and tell her about a late-night raid in her neighborhood! "Police and FBI and immigration law enforcement people were all over the place, like a scene out of a movie. Guns were out, pointed at the house; all the doors were open and lights were on. Then a short, stout man came out in a tee shirt and pants with no shoes, and his hands were cuffed behind him. The police took out computers and other things from the house, and a little while later a woman was led out in handcuffs and put into another car, and after that two Hispanic men were brought out. My heavens, you never know who you live next to!"

Hearing about the whole episode gave me the jitters. What would Jim say if he knew about any of this?

That night Jim and I were watching the movie "Clear and Present Danger" on TV and I took the opportunity to ask him a question. "Jim, what would you do if you knew something, and you find out that the only way you could get justice done is to testify against someone you know?"

"Depends on the crime, I guess."

"Would you stand up for what is right?"

I could tell by his face that he knew something was wrong. "Yes, I would testify against a person I knew." Then he wanted to know why I was wondering about it.

But I had my answer. I went to bed that night and woke up refreshed for the first time in months. I had come to a decision. Jim had no idea he had helped me make up my mind about testifying.

What happened next was kind of funny. Jim woke up and turned to me with a smile and said that all night I practically nudged him out of bed. "No matter how much I pushed you away, you were always right there."

"Oh, gosh, I'm sorry."

"You were also talking in your sleep. You kept saying, 'Stop. Stop."

"I guess it was some kind of dream," I said quickly. But I knew what it really was; I wanted the whole situation at the bank to just stop!

At work in the morning Carol told me that all the tellers at the main branch had all been replaced, and there was new protocol at work. Everything would be tightly run. Overnight. Now, no one could do anything without two signatures. Tellers could not go into the vault without three people present. All paperwork was kept under lock and key by the chief operating officer, not in the vault where anyone could grab something while they were getting a safety deposit box or a teller drawer.

And if anyone had an affair with a bank employee, one or both would be fired.

Chapter Fourteen

In the middle of this muddle, I admitted to myself that my lost diamond would never be found. Jim could tell I was feeling low, but he had no idea what was really weighing on my mind. He thought it was my missing diamond.

One Saturday he took me to the jewelry store downtown where we looked at many different diamonds. He wanted a perfect one, like the one he'd picked out for my engagement ring. The jeweler showed us lots of stones, but Jim kept shaking his head no. Little did I know he had talked to the jeweler before we arrived, and we were picking out not one diamond but *three*—a large stone for the center with slightly smaller diamonds on either side.

The jeweler positioned three diamonds all together in a gold band, and I ooh'd and aah'd. Jim said, "Yes, that's it!"

I looked up at him. "Really?" I was taken completely by surprise. Three diamonds?

The jeweler then had Jim and me wait while he went to set the diamonds in place on my new wedding band. When we got home, I carefully laid my original wedding ring, minus the lost diamond, in my jewelry case.

Monday morning I had an early meeting at the main branch. I hadn't been in the office for 10 minutes before Deanna said loudly, "Is your ring real?" I thought she looked just a tad jealous.

I moved away from her and walked over to Carol's desk. She took one look at my new ring and said, "Nice! That's some husband you have!"

The next morning Scott and Sara admired my sparkly new diamond ring. "Your ring comes at a good time to cheer you up," Sara said.

Scott looked right at Sara. "My wife loves jewelry." Sara quickly put her hand in her lap.

It was the first time I'd heard anything personal expressed by either Scott or Sara. And then I had a question: How did they stay away from their spouses for this length of time? Suddenly I wondered if maybe their spouses were here, with them; maybe they'd been here all along? Maybe their families were right here in town?

But I didn't dare ask.

Scott clammed up right after he made that comment, and to my surprise Sara looked at him as if he'd done something wrong.

Then I had a niggle of intuition. I bet Scott and Sara were married! I tried to fish around for information, but they told me to leave it alone. So I did.

I would never know for sure, but I think they were.

At our next meeting at the bakery, I told Scott and Sara that I had decided to testify against Joel. "Not because I want to do this," I said, "but because it is the right thing to do."

They both looked relieved. "We'll do everything humanly possible to keep you out of the courthouse," Scott assured me.

I tried to smile. I was sure going to need my doctor's prescription for anti-anxiety medication.

"We're almost finished with this case," Scott said. "With your testimony, things should go like clockwork."

I looked at them both. "You've been here for so long! Don't you have homes and families?"

Neither one answered.

At the bank that morning I opened the branch and then Carol arrived. "Laura is home sick today, so it's just us."

"Okay," I said.

"Everything sure feels different, doesn't it?" she remarked. I knew exactly what she meant. Then she told me that some of the tellers had left to go to other banks and she would have to hire two more.

"Do you have any nice friends like you who might want a job?"

I looked at her and smiled. "I'll think about it." But I knew I would never, *never* ask any of my friends to work in this place. Not after what I'd just gone through . . . and still had yet to endure.

The week before I had to testify, Jim and I and the kids had to fly to Minneapolis for a family funeral. One of the FBI agents flew with us. It was

Scott. Jim never knew. I was told later that we had been followed by several agents because I was a star witness, and the FBI didn't want anything to happen to me. From the time we landed in Minneapolis, the police had undercover agents watching our every move and protecting us. Creepy.

The night after we got home, the phone rang. "Friday I need you at the courthouse at one o'clock sharp," Scott announced. "Open up the Westville branch; then Carol will cover for you."

Oh, no. *It's too soon for this.* How I wished I could change my mind! The rest of the night was a blur, and the days until Friday were the longest days I could ever remember. Oh, Lord, I just wanted to get this whole thing over with.

Thursday night I got another phone call. "Scott here. Meet us at the bakery first thing tomorrow morning."

What was going on? I couldn't ask him anything within Jim's hearing, so I just sweated. Maybe they were going to prompt me about what to say?

I didn't sleep that night. The next morning I got the kids to school and made it to the bakery just in time. I decided to go inside with an open mind and not expect the worst. Besides, I thought, what else could possibly happen now?

Scott gestured at an empty chair. "Have a seat, Rose."

"What's up?" I asked.

"You are one of the luckiest people ever," he said.

I stared at him, then at Sara. "Why? What happened?"

"Yesterday in court they showed Joel the photos you took of the vault and the ATM. He cracked and admitted to stealing money and taking property that belonged to the bank. And . . . " For some reason he looked over at Carol. "He also confessed to a murder."

For a minute I couldn't say anything. "Are you serious? Really?"

"We also have more damning information about Joel and his brother and others that we won't mention, who were involved with drugs. Joel had a drug problem; that's what started this whole thing. Rose, it's over."

"Over? You mean *all* over?"

"All over. Joel was sentenced to 25 years in federal prison. Seven other people were implicated and sentenced as well."

I started to cry.

"You can go to work and not worry about this anymore. You won't have to testify. It's finished. Thank God you took those photographs; that was the evidence that turned Joel and Fredric and Miles against each other."

"Did Carol have to testify?"

"No."

"Thank God."

Sara took my hand. "I'd like to officially thank you for your upstanding, honest behavior throughout this whole ordeal. We could not have done this without your dedication."

I was still crying, and both of them were smiling at me. "Good job, Mrs. Ryan," Scott said. "You've made it through a terrible episode. I hope you'll try hard to forget this ever happened."

"Does this mean I can finally tell my husband?"

They both looked down at the table.

"Oh, no," I groaned.

"The best thing would be for you to forget this," Scott said soberly.

"But I've been lying to my husband and my kids all this time. When can I tell them?"

Scott frowned. "Maybe you can talk about it in twenty-five years, when everyone has served their time."

Sara leaned over and said, "I hope you will have forgotten all this by then."

"So this is our last meeting?"

"Yes," Scott said. "We are extremely happy to say this is our last meeting. Walk out that door and don't look back."

Everything seemed different when I drove to work. The trees looked greener, the sunshine brighter. Finally, *finally* this was all behind me.

Laura was at the bank when I arrived. "Hello," I said. "How are you doing this morning?"

"You heard?"

"Heard what?"

"We have two new tellers at the main branch."

"No, I hadn't heard that Carol hired anyone yet."

No sooner had we opened the branch than Carol was standing in the lobby. "Hello, Rose. Could I have a minute of your time?"

"Sure." We walked to the front of the office, out of sight of Laura and the security cameras, and she turned to me. "Congratulations, Rose. As of this morning, you are the new manager of the Westville branch."

"What?" I was flabbergasted.

"It's official. The new president, Mr. Squires, will announce it this afternoon." I hugged her, and I knew that *she* knew what I was really hugging her about. I couldn't speak, so we just grinned at each other.

"This comes with a pay raise and official responsibility, which you have already proven you are capable of."

I sighed. "I can't believe what has happened this past year."

"Me, either. It's sure been a long one!"

"Now what?" I asked.

"Get in there and just do your job."

"Carol?"

She turned to me. "Good luck to the two of us," I said. "We did a good thing."

On a wild hunch I went to the computer and Googled Claire's name. An obituary notice popped it. It said the family had held a private burial for the untimely death of their daughter. The date given was the month I came to work at the Westville branch.

Chapter Fifteen

I drove home in a daze. "Hello, everyone. I'm home!"

Jim came up behind me. "Someone just called you."

"Who?"

"Your doctor."

"Did I forget an appointment?"

"No. She wants you to make several appointments, actually." He was looking at me intently.

"What do you mean? What for?"

"Rose, you're pregnant."

"WHAAT?"

"The doctor wanted you to know right away, and since you had the miscarriage last year, she wants to monitor you closely."

After a long, long embrace, I finally looked up at him. "So this is why my stomach has been upset. Oh, Jim, this is wonderful news! I haven't been this happy in a long time.

And . . . " I took a deep breath " . . . do you want to hear something else?"

"What could top this?" he said.

"Today I was officially named manager of the Westville branch!"

"That's wonderful, too," my husband said. "Good for you, honey."

We kept my pregnancy secret until I was three months along. I didn't tell them at work until I was almost six months along, and then I developed complications and ended up on bed rest for the rest of my pregnancy. I felt as if a larger force was trying to tell me something.

When Anne was born I decided I would stay home for at least three months after her delivery. But during that time I gradually began to realize I couldn't go back to work at all. I'd made it through one of the worst years of my life, and my reward was this wonderful baby girl. I had to remain at home.

When I made the decision, I called Carol.

"Congratulations on your new baby, Rose. How are you feeling?"

"Great. But . . ." I swallowed. "Jim and I have come to a decision. I'm not coming back to the bank. I've decided to stay home with the baby."

"I'm not surprised," Carol said slowly. "But if you ever change your mind, you are welcome back any time. Just say the word."

"I will, Carol. Thanks. And Carol?"

"Yes?"

"How are *you* doing now that the whole mess is over?"

"I'm good, Rose. Very good. I have a new husband, and I've been promoted to vice president of the bank."

We hung up the phone, both of us happy. I had little Anne in my arms and life seemed just perfect.

Chapter Sixteen

27 Years Later

My mother had worked as a decoder in the CIA during World War II. During her last years, I know things about her experiences bubbled up, but she never talked about them. I will never know exactly what Mom did, but I do know that on her deathbed she was haunted by it.

Twenty-seven years after my experience at the Harvest Bank, my mother's death dredged up my memories about the time at the bank. By then my three children were grown and had children of their own. After my mother's death I decided it was finally time to tell Jim about what I had been involved in at the bank.

I remember that day well. It was a Saturday morning, and Jim and I went out to get morning coffee and then had plans to go out for lunch. We were both busy working away on our laptop computers and I thought about finally sharing my secret life.

We drove to a restaurant on the north end of town where we sat across from each other, talking about the kids, and what was going on with our grandkids.

"Jim, remember when I worked at Harvest Bank?"

"Yes. It was right before we had Anne. They really liked you there."

"Yes." I started to fidget. Then slowly I started to talk.

"I haven't been able to tell you something that happened during those years because I was told not to say anything to anyone, not even you."

Jim looked up at me with a puzzled expression. "What happened, Rose?"

I started at the beginning. "Remember those tellers I used to talk about?"

"The girls that always went bar-hopping?"

"Yes." I took in a deep, deep breath. "Remember the day I was asked to go over to the Westville branch?"

"Yes. I remember you were a wreck a good deal of the time after you did."

"It was stressful," I said. "And now I want to tell you why."

Jim was suddenly all attention.

"That first day I started working at the little branch, I discovered a $40,000 shortage."

"I don't remember you saying anything about that," he said. Then his eyes widened. "What did you do?"

"I had Margaret's little camera in my purse, and I took photos of the vault and the ATM receipts. It was the only thing I could think of to do to protect myself."

He got a funny look on his face. "Yes? What happened then?"

"The manager kept saying what a good day it was, but that day I noticed he opened a lot of accounts and left them in his desk drawer. He didn't bother to process them. And I knew something was wrong."

"Wrong," Jim said slowly.

"Yes. I got nervous about having that $100,000 shortage show up on *my* record. I thought I'd better tell someone about it. So I ended up telling the president of the bank."

Jim laid down his fork and stared at me. "And?"

"When I started to tell the president, I noticed he was uneasy. He told me not to tell anyone, that he would take care of the problem."

"And?" Jim said again.

"He wasn't acting right, and I knew something was wrong. I left his office, but as I was closing the door behind me I overheard him on the phone with my manager, and he said, 'Rose knows. Now we have to get her the hell out of there!'"

I took a gulp from my water glass. "Jim, I was scared to death. I didn't know what to do, but I knew I had to do *something*."

Jim was still staring at me. "So, what did you do?"

"I drove straight to the police station."

"You went to the police? Wait a minute, *you went to the police?*"

"Yes."

100

The oddest look came into his eyes. "What happened? What did they say?"

"An officer sat me down and had me tell him what I knew. So I told him about the vault and the huge loss, and then I told him about what I'd overheard the president of the bank say on the phone.

"The police officer said he needed to call in the FBI and I nearly fainted. He took all kinds of information about our cars, make and model, and license plate numbers. And from then on you, Margaret, Anthony, and I were followed by undercover police."

"What? We were all followed?"

"Yes. He said it was for our own safety."

Jim was sitting closer to me now, listening intently.

"That night someone from the FBI called and said to meet him the next morning at the Sweet Treat Bakery. I couldn't tell you. I couldn't tell the kids. From that moment on I was a psychological mess."

"Did you go to the bakery?"

"Yes. Two people, a man and later a woman, pulled out their FBI badges and showed them to me. I thought I would pass out."

Jim took my hand and held it. "What happened next?"

"They told me what I needed to do."

"And that was?"

"I had to start compiling evidence for them, account numbers, the amount of money the branch was short, the amount of money that should be in the accounts. They had me put copies of the paperwork in a magazine and hand it over at our meetings at the bakery. The worst part was I was told to stay at the Westville branch because they wanted to stop the manager—his name was Joel—in his tracks, and I was the key."

"Did you succeed?"

"Well, at first I thought I would, but things got more and more complicated. Joel had a brother who would come into the bank every day and hang around. It turned out he was stealing new account information, along with money, and he took it out of the bank hidden inside a newspaper. It was shocking to watch, and he, or Joel, kept disabling the security cameras so he wouldn't be discovered. I later learned he had a drug problem."

Jim just stared at me. I kept talking.

"When the FBI came in, they bugged the whole bank, so I was watched and listened to all day long. It was nerve-racking, but they needed to watch Joel like a hawk. He was nuts. And dangerous."

"Dangerous?" Jim folded and refolded his napkin. "What do you mean, dangerous?"

"Jim, this is the part I'm scared to tell you."

He leaned farther toward me and took my hand. "Go on, tell me."

I took a deep breath and told him about the day I saw that Joel carried a gun.

"A gun! Oh, honey, I would have gotten you out of there so fast . . . I might have even moved us out of the area." When he reached for his coffee I saw that his hand was shaking.

"I know. And so did the FBI agents. They kept telling me I had to keep what was going on secret for everyone's safety. It was hard, Jim. Awfully hard. Every day when I got home from work I wanted to tell you all the stuff that was going on, but I couldn't. I knew it could be dangerous for you and for the kids."

Jim put his arm around my shoulders and hugged me tight. "Did your guys nail the manager?"

"Yes, finally. I have to tell you there are things I will never know about that case, even though I was in the thick of it. I compiled lists of documents and gave them to the FBI agents to sort out; when the vault was short, they brought in money so the bank would balance. To this day I don't know where that money came from. I don't know why I ever thought of taking those photographs that first day."

"What photographs?"

"Remember when Margaret was doing that biology field study report and I lost her photos? I didn't lose them. The FBI confiscated them because the camera I used also had my photos of the vault and the ATM records. Those photos were what sealed Joel's fate. And that's why the FBI worked so hard to keep me safe—I was their informant."

"Good God. But they did arrest the manager, right?"

"Yes, they did. And then they told me I'd have to testify in court."

Jim looked at me and shook his head. "Why? They had tons of evidence by then."

"I was the star witness."

"How many people ended up being involved?"

"I think a total of seven, including two bank presidents if you can believe it. The FBI agents told me just the minimum, for my own safety."

"Was there a trial?"

"Oh, yes. Joel got twenty-five years."

"Good! What finally happened with the bank?"

"People started getting fired. Many tellers were let go because of inter-office affairs. I don't know if any of those people were part of the embezzling scheme."

Finally Jim leaned back and said quietly, "So that's why you wanted to stay home after you had Anne?"

"I couldn't go back to the bank, even after I was offered the branch manager position. My heart wasn't in it. And I was still scared. Now you know why my anxiety level was so high."

Jim huffed out a laugh. "My God, Rose, I thought maybe you'd inherited your mother's tendency toward anxiety. I never dreamed you had to go to work every day and worry about people with guns who were stealing money. That was dangerous!"

I felt like crying right then and there. "It was so dangerous it literally made me sick. The FBI agents scared me to death talking about what might happen if I told anyone—even you—about what was going on. So I didn't. And later, when I found out everything *else* that was involved, things the FBI wouldn't tell me, I was even more scared."

Jim just shook his head. "It all makes sense now. Everything. What made you decide to tell me all this now?"

I took a deep breath. "I thought that, after twenty-seven years had passed, I could finally tell you without worrying that someone would come to find me. There was always the threat of having to testify against Joel. I was a nervous wreck about that. It wasn't until the week after the raid that Joel confessed to everything and implicated the others. That's when I found out he had a drug problem."

"Wow, Rose," he said slowly. "My wife was an FBI informant!"

"I guess. They never called me that, but I did work with them to get Joel and the others convicted."

"Call it what you want, Rose, but that's exactly what you were—an FBI informant. My God . . . " He gave a short laugh " . . . you never know who you're sleeping with!"

"I never thought of myself as an informant. Never."

Jim kept shaking his head, and then he looked at me with an expression in his eyes I'd never seen before. "It took courage to do what you did, honey. I'm proud of you."

I started to cry, and Jim put his arm around me. "I don't have any idea what I would have done in your situation," he said. He thought a minute and started to smile. "What happened to the bar-hopping girls you told me about?"

I choked out a laugh. "I ran into the teller who used to call me Mary Poppins, you know the one who was looking for Mr. Right in bars? Deanna, that's her name. She's still single, but she's not working in banks anymore. Gerri, the other teller, got pregnant on a trip to Hawaii with Deanna. Gerri cheated on her husband and he left her, so now she lives out of state with her mother and her son."

"Not surprising," Jim said.

"I did run into Joel after his prison term was up. It was very awkward. He said he'd been on an 'extended vacation.' Just knowing he was still in town scared me out of saying anything to you."

Jim just nodded.

"You know what?" I said. "What happened changed how I felt about being out in public. I didn't realize until later that I started to withdraw from everything, the Junior Women's Club, my church group, everything. I was afraid I'd let something slip. And . . . " I gave a little laugh

" . . . you know how reluctant I've always been to use the computer? Well, that police officer warned me about the risks in putting yourself out there for crazy people to find out things about you. I guess I've been worried all these years about someone coming after us."

Jim just sat there. "Wow. *Wow*. Rose, you have to tell the kids about this."

"You really think I should? Believe me, it's been tough to keep all this secret from you.

"Why not tell them? You should be proud of what you did."

I thought for a long minute. "But, Jim, where do I begin?"

He gave me the sweetest smile. "Rose, honey, just tell them when it all began—the morning you had breakfast with the FBI."

So I did.

Afterword

Telling Jim about the FBI ordeal was a huge relief for me. It also stirred up a lot of emotions, and I can't underplay how frightening the whole thing was. It turned my life upside down and then some.

I tried to get over my fear and anxiety by repressing it, but when my mom died, those feelings returned with a vengeance. I was nervous every time I ran into one of the bank's former employees. I thought I was coping just fine, but now I can see I was masking a lot of anxiety.

Letting Jim and the kids know what I did, and that it was something really important, was an uplifting experience. I always knew Jim was disappointed when I decided to stay home with Anne and put a promising career behind me. Now he understands that I was protecting myself and my family in the only way I could. The thought of a gun in my bank manager's hands was so overwhelmingly frightening I knew I could never again take such a risk.

To this day, Jim talks about my experience with pride. I know that no one will ever know where this occurred, or who is who. Maybe it doesn't matter any longer. The FBI agents were right; I did forget about all of it, for a while at least, until my mother was dying and her untold stories about what she had done in World War II triggered memories of what I had done almost 70 years later.

Jim and our kids now look at me a lot differently. They know I was a successful business woman with great common sense who stood up for what was right and in the end, when push came to shove, I weighed the prospect of a career in banking against being with my family and I chose my family. It was the right thing to do.

Appendix: What Happened Much Later

Many years later, I ran into Deanna. She looked a lot older, even haggard. Apparently she still liked to drink. She said she was here visiting her mother, who was in her nineties and in poor health. Deanna still lived in the area but not in Westville, and she confided that she hasn't worked in banking since I last saw her. I knew she could never be bonded again and would never be able to work around money. She didn't let on that she had gone to prison, and of course I didn't ask.

A month later I saw Gerri in front of a local drugstore. She was driving an old, beat-up car, and she told me she lived with her mother and had had a son. She said she and Deanna had taken a vacation together and Gerri had hooked up with a man for a one-night stand and ended up pregnant. She then said that her husband at that time couldn't father children and he had left her because of it. Why she told me this I have no idea.

She astounded me by confessing it was one of two regrets in her life, and of course I wondered if the other regret was the bank scheme all those years ago. I felt sorry for her, and I didn't say anything about my family. I didn't want her to know anything about me or about Jim and our kids. It was very sad.

Then one cool winter morning about six months later I was at a local coffee shop reading the newspaper when I looked up and almost fainted. Fredric and Kallie were sitting two tables away. Kallie had her arm around him and he was leaning in close to her.

Kallie looked at me and did a double-take. Instantly she moved away from Fredric, and then he saw me, too. Kallie started up a conversation, and I quickly told myself not to say anything about my family. *Nothing.*

She said she was happily married to someone named Charles. But good Lord, she was obviously still involved with Fredric!

Fredric said he lived out of state someplace and that he was here visiting old friends. He also said he'd been on 'an extended vacation.' Of course I knew he'd been in prison for many years.

I said I was late for a meeting and got up to leave, but I was sweating. I managed not to say much of anything about myself, but I sure got an earful from them. And their behavior toward one another made what they didn't say very obvious.

But the worst encounter was yet to come. One sunny day I decided to go shopping downtown and was just locking my car door when I got a glimpse of Joel. I almost didn't see him at first, but he looked right at me. I wanted to run away.

"Hello, Rose," he said.

I managed to nod. "Joel." I tried not to come to a complete stop, but kept moving.

"I've been on an extended vacation," he said. "I moved out of state and I just came back to visit my mother's grave. I haven't been here in years."

Oh my God, I thought, he'll see my car license plate! *Get out of here. Get out of here!*

I kept moving, walked past him, smiling and perspiring. I turned the corner and stood there almost paralyzed from the encounter. Suddenly I was afraid all over again. I had to get home.

I walked around the corner for a few minutes, then forgot all about shopping and went back to my car. More than 25 years had passed and I still had this panicked reaction? I needed to know if he had really moved out of the area.

I went to the library to use their computer; I was afraid to go home and even type his name into my own! In a minute the information popped up across the screen. Yes, he actually did live out of state.

What a relief. I decided it was just a chance encounter. A bit calmer by then, I typed in Miles's name, and there it was: Deceased.

Thank you, God. *Thank you!*

It is really hard to do the right thing when it's looking you in the face. It's especially hard when it could be dangerous, not just for you but for your family.

From that day on, I never cease to give thanks for my life, and for the lives of those I love.